Douglas SBD dive-bombers attack on the *Akagi* in the Battle of Midway, June 4, 1942.

W9-ARH-196

AGGRESSORS

VOLUME
2

CARRIER POWER
VS.
FIGHTING SHIP

Text by NORMAN POLMAR

Illustrations by RIKYU WATANABE

Twin 25 mm Type 96 anti-aircraft machine gun mount in the Japanese battleship *Nagato*, autumn of 1941. (Yoji Watanabe)

40 mm Bofors anti-aircraft machine guns in quadruple mounting in the USS *Lexington* (CV-16), November 1943. (National Archives)

Frontispiece: Vought Corsair IIs on board the *Victorious* belonged to the Royal Navy Eastern Fleet on September 18, 1944. These fighters prepare to launch against a Japanese railway repair and maintenance center at Sigli in Sumatra. (Imperial War Museum)

Copyright © 1990 by Zokeisha Publications Ltd., Tokyo/New York. All rights reserved.
Edited by Yoji Watanabe.

First published in the United States of America by Howell Press, Inc., 700 Harris Street, Suite B, Charlottesville, Virginia 22901.
Telephone (804) 977-4006.

This book, or any portions thereof, may not be reproduced or transmitted in any form or by any means, electronic or mechanical, including photocopying, recording, or by any information storage and retrieval system, without permission in writing from the publisher.

Library of Congress Catalog Card Number 89-82171
ISBN 0-943231-32-9
Printed in Japan.
First printing
HOWELL PRESS

Note: All 'miles' in the main text are referred to as nautical miles'

Building for War

During the Second World War two ships emerged as the dominant naval weapons—the aircraft carrier and the submarine. The aircraft carrier developed during the conflict into a highly effective, far-ranging weapon that could engage enemy fleets, attack enemy forces and installations on land, and survive in the face of the most effective defenses possible. The carrier concepts that emerged in the war have survived for more than four decades, forming the basis of the modern U.S. aircraft carrier force and, probably, the carrier fleet now being constructed by the Soviet Union.

In contrast, the submarine evolved little during the war. Development of the snorkel underwater breathing tube and submarine radar certainly improved submarine capabilities, as did the German development of high-speed hull forms and improved diesel-electric propulsion brought together in the Type XXI U-boat. But the submarine that went to sea in September 1939 and that of May 1945 had the same basic capabilities and limitations, and the countermeasures to defeat them existed. This was not true of aircraft carriers. The carriers and their aircraft as well as their tactics changed significantly during the conflict. They became the most effective ship killers of the war.

Perhaps most important, the submarine, armed with deck guns and torpedoes, had a striking range measured in hundreds or, at best, thousands of yards. The aircraft carrier could launch bombers that could strike out against targets hundreds of miles away—targets afloat or on land.

The beginnings of the aircraft carrier are shrouded in the romantic beginnings of manned flight. As early as 1898, American scientist Samuel P. Langley experimented—unsuccessfully—with catapulting flying machines from barges.

The first successful manned flight is credited to the Americans Orville and Wilbur Wright, who flew—a distance of 40 yards (37 m)—over the beaches of North Carolina in 1903. Immediately military officers began looking at the implications of their flying machine for war. When Orville Wright conducted demonstration flights for the U.S. Army near Washington, D.C., in September of 1908 two U.S. naval officers were present. To most Navy personnel the flying machine was viewed as a means of extending an observer's sight beyond that possible from a masthead. Two years later American aviation pioneer Glenn Curtiss flew one of his home-built machines over a lake in New York where floats had been arranged in the outline of a 500 ft by 90 ft (152 m by 27 m) battleship. Dropping eight-inch (20 cm) lengths of steel pipe on the floats, Curtiss awakened many to the potential of an airplane attacking a ship at sea.

Of course, dropping steel pipes on floats would be far different than attacking a warship at sea, although the press saw the matter quite simply: *The New York Times* declared a new "menace to the armored fleets of the war." The controversy of airplane versus fleets was thus begun before the U.S. Navy or Royal Navy had a single airplane (the U.S. Army had one flying machine at the time).

The principal problem for navies was how to have an airplane take off from a ship and, after flying its mission, land back on board. In Novermber 1910 the U.S. Navy—still without an airplane of its own—attacked that problem. Curtiss provided the airplane and, flown by Eugene B. Ely, an exhibition pilot for Curtiss, the biplane made a remarkable take off from a platform installed over the bow of the light cruiser *Birmingham*, anchored in Chesapeake Bay, and then flew to a nearby airfield.

The following January, Ely flew a biplane from a field near San Francisco to land on a wooden platform erected over the stern of the armored cruiser *Pennsylvania*. To stop the plane on the sloped, 119 1/3 ft (36.4 m) wooden platform, the Navy had arranged 22 pairs of 50 lb (23 kg) sandbags at three-foot (0.9 m) intervals, each pair connected by a line stretched taught 12 in (30 cm) above the deck. With hooks fitted to his plane, Ely skimmed low over the deck and successfully landed aboard, establishing another first while introducing the aircraft arresting concept that survives to this day.

(More feasible, in the view of senior U.S. naval officers, was the use of flying boats from ships. They could be catapulted off and, coming down in the water alongside, be hoisted back on board by crane.)

The Royal Navy repeated the Ely flying-off trials in the winter of 1911–1912, with Lieutenant Charles R. Samson successfully taking off from platforms erected on several battleships. Late in 1912 the old light cruiser *Hermes* was commissioned as a parent ship for naval aircraft, being albe to carry two floatplanes that were launched on trolleys from a short flying deck built over her bow. The planes on board *Hermes* were fitted with folding wings, an idea of the First Lord of the Admiralty, Winston S. Churchill, who also called planes that could alight on water simply "seaplanes" instead of by the previous term "hydroaeroplanes."

When the First World War erupted in August 1914 the fledgling Royal Naval Air Service (RNAS) moved rapidly to exploit the use of the airplane in the war at sea. Several cross-Channel steamers were each modified to carry four seaplanes for coastal patrol. For use with the fleet, the old Cunard liner *Campania* was fitted with a flying-off deck some 120 ft (37 m) over her bow, with provisions for carrying ten seaplanes. But the early combat flights by the RNAS were flown mostly from bases on the continent. (Beyond using airplanes for reconnaissance, the RNAS operated armored cars in this role, with one such "squadron" seeing action in Russia!)

Based in Belgium, the RNAS planes also conducted bombing missions against German Zeppelin bases. Early on

Sopwith Pup fighter made the first flight from the aft turret of the battlecruiser *Repulse* on October 14, 1917. (Imperial War Museum)

Christmas Day 1914 the Royal Navy pilots carried out history's first ship-based air strike. From three of the converted cross-Channel steamers, seven seaplanes were lowered by crane into the water and took off to bomb the German base of Cuxhaven. Low clouds and anti-aircraft fire forced the British planes to miss hitting the airship sheds. Two similar ship-based raids against the airship sheds also ended in failure.

But seaplane carrier operations continued, and in late May 1916 the seaplane carrier *Engadine* flew reconnaissance in the early stages of the Battle of Jutland. Howere, the limited capability of the aircraft, delays in radio transmissions, and the British fleet commander's lack of understanding of the potential of aircraft caused the carrier's aircraft to have no affect on the battle.

Still, procedures were established and more successful floatplane operations, both reconnaissance and bombing, were soon being flown from British seaplane carriers operating off the Turkish coast. One British seaplane made history's first aerial torpedo attack, sinking a Turkish ship in the Sea of Marmara. These seaplane and seaplane carrier operations, and the flying off of fighters from platforms on battleship turrets and from platforms towed behind destroyers, were invaluable in giving the Royal Navy the experience necessary to develop true aircraft carriers.

The first carrier for wheeled aircraft was the battle cruiser *Furious*, taken in hand before completion and fitted with a flying off deck forward while retaining a single 18 in (45.7 cm) gun aft. Completed in July 1917, the 19,100-ton ship could steam at 31 $\frac{1}{2}$ knots. Initially the *Furious* carried four seaplanes and six wheeled aircraft, with a hydraulic-operated lift to transport them between hangar and flight decks.

Although the forward deck of the *Furious* was intended only for takeoffs, almost immediately experiments were conducted with an aircraft flying slowly over the deck and, with men running to grab pull-down straps, bringing the biplanes back aboard. These experiments—some fatal—led to a further modification of the ship: the 18 in (45.7 cm) gun, the largest afloat, was deleted and a flying-on deck was installed aft. Thus

refitted, the ship had flight decks at both ends, separated by a large superstructure, including a funnel sprewing hot exhaust that interferred with approaching planes. Trackways permitted moving planes between the flight decks.

Thus configured, in July 1918 the *Furious* flew the first aircraft carrier strike, sending seven Camel fighters to bomb the Zeppelin sheds at Tondern. Two sheds, each containing a Zeppelin, were destroyed. The loss, however, of five planes—all of their pilots survived—with the two "surviving" planes having to come down at sea near the *Furious*, caused the British navy to halt flights from the ship. She served the remainder of the war as a tender for observation balloons.

Meanwhile, British shipyards were at work converting and building aircraft carriers. A light cruiser was completed as the carrier *Vindictive* (9,750 tons), and a liner being built for Italy was completed as the carrier *Argus* (15,775 tons), both joining the fleet in 1918. A dreadnought battleship that was being built for Chile was completed in 1920 as the carrier *Eagle* (22,600 tons), and the *Hermes*—the world's first ship laid down for the purpose of an aircraft carrier—was finished in 1923 (10,850 tons).

These four ships—plus the *Furious*, the largest of the lot—had very different configurations and operating characteristics, which provided the British with considerable operating experience. This coupled with the experience of naval aviation in the war and the excellence of wartime British aircraft provided the basis for strong carrier development between the wars. But it was not to be. On April 1, 1918—All Fool's Day—the Royal Naval Air Service became part of the new Royal Air Force (RAF), which took control of all flying military activities and aircraft development. It would be a devastating blow to British carrier aviation and the leadership in this important aspect of naval development shift to Japan and the United States.

Japanese naval aviation had its beginnings in 1912, when naval officers were sent to France and the United States (the Curtiss school) for flight instruction. One of the young officers was Lieutenant Chikuhei Nakajima, later the founder of the aircraft company that carried his name. Using foreign-

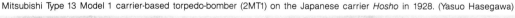

Mitsubishi Type 13 Model 1 carrier-based torpedo-bomber (2MT1) on the Japanese carrier *Hosho* in 1928. (Yasuo Hasegawa)

USS *Langley* (CV-1) with her full complement of 34 aircraft on the flight deck. (National Archives)

built aircraft, the naval air service was established upon their return, and in the fall of 1913 the naval transport *Wakamiya-Maru* was modified for use with seaplane experiments. She sent off floatplanes to attack German holdings in China early in World War I. And, using naval shells modified into bombs, they sank a German minelayer.

As in the Royal Navy, the Japanese experimented with flying airplanes from platforms atop gun turrets, and after considerable study and design efforts, in December 1919 the carrier *Hosho* was begun, second only to the British *Hermes* as a purpose-built carrier. The Japanese ship, however, was completed first, in December 1922. The *Hosho* (7,470 tons), could accommodate 21 aircraft of various types.

The United States did not enter the war until April 1917, but when it did American soldiers, marines (who fought ashore as soldiers), destroyers, and naval aircraft turned the tide in favor of the allies. (Army aviators all flew foreign aircraft in combat.) After the conflict ended the Navy gave serious consideration to various means of taking airplanes to sea. Eight battleships had platforms built over gun turrets for flying-off wheeled airplanes, and there were considerable seaplane activities.

In 1919 an unfinished merchant ship was acquired for conversion to an airship and seaplane tender (to be named *Wright*), and a collier, built in 1913, was taken into a yard for conversion to a flush-deck carrier. She emerged in 1922 as the *Langley* (CV-1) of 11,050 tons, the first of a long line of U.S. aircraft carriers.

Most significant for the future of carrier aviation, the navies of both Japan and the United States kept their own air arms; Britain, Germany, and Italy all established single air forces to control all military aviation—a fatal flaw for the future development of carrier aviation.

The French Navy in 1912 converted the torpedo boat carrier *Foundre* to carry seaplanes. With a pair of aircraft in 1913 she had been the first ship of any navy to provide ship-based aircraft in fleet maneuvers. Later a plane was flown off from a platform built over her bow. The *Foundre* served in the eastern Mediterranean during the war, with three cross-Channel steamers also being configured to carry seaplanes.

After the war the major naval powers sought agreements to slow the massive, expensive warship construction programs. After extensive negotiations in Washington, D.C., a naval arms limitation treaty was agreed to in February 1922. The treaty defined limits for capital ships and aircraft carriers of the signatory nations. The existing aircraft carriers were considered as experimental ships and not counted against quotas.

The new carriers were defined as ships over 10,000 tons standard displacement, not to exceed 27,000 tons except that each nation could have up to two ships of 33,000 tons, which could be converted from battleships or battle cruisers that would otherwise be disposed of under the treaty's terms. This later point would provide the basis for some of the most interesting and important carriers of World War II. The Royal Navy converted the "light" battle cruisers *Courageous* and *Glorious* (22,500 tons); the Japanese completed a battle cruiser and a battleship as the *Akagi* and *Kaga*, respectively (26,900 tons); and the United States completed a pair of large battle cruisers as the nominal 33,000-ton *Lexington* (CV-2) and *Saratoga* (CV-3). The American ships were actually larger— about 37,680 tons standard—but U.S. admirals claimed that the additional tonnage was for "equipment for defense against air and submarine attack," which was allowed for under the treaty.

These ships were the largest "flattops" of the between-war period, and all saw considerable action. Only one of these six ships, the USS *Saratoga*, would survive the coming war. These ships provided their respective navies with rich operating experience between the wars.

All three navies subsequently embarked on the construction of purpose-built carriers within the limitations of the Washington treaty. Both the United States and Japan undertook major programs to develop both carriers and specialized aircraft to fly from them. The first new U.S. carrier was the small *Ranger* (CV-4) of only 14,500 tons. Joining the fleet in 1934, she was the result of many cost-reduction efforts; she was small with a limited aircraft capacity, no facilities for storing torpedoes, and slow speed (29 1/2 knots compared to 33 knots for most other U.S. carriers).

Much more successful were the next ships, the *Yorktown* (CV-5) and *Enterprise* (CV-6) of 19,900 tons, completed in 1937 and 1938. Then, to use up the remaining treaty tonnage, the United States built the smaller *Wasp* (CV-7) of 14,700 tons. With the end of the naval treaty limitations, a last prewar carrier was built to the basic *Yorktown* design, the 20,000-ton *Hornet* (CV-8). These four carriers, and the ex-battle cruisers "Lex" and "Sara" would be the backbone of the U.S. Pacific Fleet for the first half of the war in the Pacific. In the inter-war years they participated in the annual fleet exercises; in the maneuvers of 1928 the *Langley* launched a surprise air attack against Pearl Harbor. Over the next decade, in mock attacks against the Panama Canal and Hawaii, the carriers demonstrated again and again that they could make surprise at-

Naval Aero-Technical Arsenal Type 96 carrier-based torpedo-bomber (B4Y1) over the carrier *Kaga* on October 14, 1937, during the first stage of the Sino-Japanese War. (Koji Ohno)

tacks against defending forces.

The Japanese Navy followed a similar pattern of development. The small, 8,000-ton *Ryujo* was completed in 1933. Carrying only 36 planes, she too was considered insufficient and was followed by the 15,900-ton *Soryu* in 1937, the 17,300-ton *Hiryu* in 1939, and the 25,675-ton *Shokaku* and *Zuikaku* in 1941. Also, the light carrier *Zuiho* of 11,200 tons, converted from a submarine tender, became available in 1940.

In addition to participating in the arduous fleet exercises, in the late 1930s Japanese carrier pilots began gaining combat experience in the skies over China. And, while both the U.S. and Japanese navies produced some excellent (as well as mediocre) ship-based aircraft, in the A6M Zero the Japanese Navy developed the most effective fighter of its time. Entering combat over China in 1940, the Zero was the first carrier fighter that was superior to its land-based opponents since the British Sopwith series of World War I.

France and Britain lagged in both carrier and carrier aircraft development in this period. The Royal Navy was plagued by budget constraints and having the RAF control the aircraft and pilots (the Navy provided observers). The venerable *Furious* was converted to a flush-deck carrier in 1921–1925, followed by conversions of the *Courageous* and *Glorious*, completed in 1928 and 1930, respectively. It was eight years before the next carrier joined the fleet, the modern, 22,000-ton *Ark Royal* in 1938. She was followed in 1940–1941 by the four 23,000-ton ships of the *Illustrious* class, innovative in introducing heavily armored flight decks to carrier construction.

Also, the failure of the RAF to provide effective carrier aircraft had belatedly been recognized, and ship-based aircraft were being transferred from the RAF to the Navy. But it was too late to build an effective carrier air arm.

For France the situation was worse. Under the terms of the Washington treaty, an unfinished battleship was completed in 1927 as the carrier *Bearn* (21,800 tons), the smallest of the converted battleships and battle cruisers. Although the *Bearn* and the British battle cruiser conversions had about the same displacement, the British ships were longer, significantly faster, and embarked more aircraft. On the eve of World War II the French began construction of two 35,000-ton carriers, the *Joffre* and *Painleve*, but they would never be finished.

German troops invaded Poland on September 1, 1939. Two days later Britain and France declared war on Germany and Europe was again plunged into war.

The Royal Navy at War

When Britain and France declared war on Germany in response to the Nazi invasion of Poland, none of the navies involved was prepared for the conflict.

The Royal Navy entered the war with seven aircraft carriers: The new *Ark Royal*, the treaty conversions *Courageous* and *Glorious*, and oft-rebuilt *Furious*, and three small ships of World War I vintage—the *Argus, Eagle,* and *Hermes*. Their aircraft capacities were relatively small. While the *Ark Royal* embarked 18 Skua fighters and 42 Swordfish torpedo-reconnaissance aircraft, the other ships had far fewer—the *Furious* and *Eagle* had only 18 Swordfish each; the *Hermes* only nine; and no planes were assigned to the *Argus*. The *Glorious* was the only other carrier to operate fighters, with 12 carried in addition to her 36 Swordfish. (The refits and the installation of additional anti-aircraft guns had reduced the aircraft capacities of the *Furious* and *Courageous*, taking the space previously allocated to fighters.)

The aircraft themselves were outdated if not obsolete. The Skua was the Royal Navy's first monoplane, a two-seat fighter/dive bomber that was inferior in performance to U.S. and Japanese ship-based fighters. The fighters in the *Glorious* were Sea Gladiator biplanes. All carriers flew the Swordfish for reconnaissance and attack, the biplane being called the "Stringbag" because of its maze of struts and wires. The Swordfish, which had first flown in 1933, had a maximum speed of 139 mph (224 km/h) without a torpedo, again far inferior to other first-line carrier bombers.

After their declaration of war, neither Britain nor France took offensive action against Germany on land. In the air, the Royal Air Force immediately began bomber raids over Germany—dropping propaganda leaflets, whose only effect was to help the German scrap paper effort. At sea the war was very real and deadly.

The German naval high command—not expecting a war with Britain until at least 1943—was building a "balanced" fleet, to include aircraft carriers as well as a battle force and submarine fleet. The first German carrier, the *Graf Zeppelin*, was launched in 1938 with another ship planned. Thus, although unprepared for war, at the outset the German Navy began sending submarines and several surface warships to sea to prey on Allied shipping.

Fairey Swordfish torpedo-bomber landing aboard the *Argus*. (Imperial War Museum)

British merchant ship losses to U-boats began on September 3, and six days later three of the carriers went to sea to hunt for German submarines. One U-boat made a torpedo attack against the *Ark Royal*, which the carrier barely avoided, and accompanying destroyers sank the undersea craft. A few days later the *Courageous* was torpedoed by a U-boat and sunk, taking 519 of her crew to their death. With her loss the Royal Navy hastily withdrew carriers from the anti-submarine role, holding them for anticipated fleet actions and to hunt German surface raiders. After anti-raider operations in the South Atlantic, in December 1939 the *Ark Royal* raced toward Montevideo to help intercept the famous "pocket battleship" *Graf Spee* after she was damaged in a fight with British cruisers. But rumors that the carrier was already just over the horizon reached the *Graf Spee*'s captain, and he scuttled his ship in the outer harbor. For the time being the *Ark Royal* was cheated of the opportunity of sending her aircraft against a major enemy warship.

The so-called "phony war" ended on April 8, 1940, when German forces invaded Denmark and Norway. The British fleet immediately went to sea to attack German warships and transports off Norwegian ports. On April 10 the *Ark Royal* launched 16 Skua fighter-bombers on a bombing run that would require a round trip of 660 miles (1,220 km), almost the limit of their range.

Taking the Germans by surprise, the 16 Skuas found the cruiser *Königsberg*, which had been earlier damaged by Norwegian shore batteries, moored to a mole. One after another the carrier planes dived, each releasing a single 500 lb (227 kg) bomb. Three bombs were direct hits and 11 were close misses. Shattered by the bombs the 6,000-ton cruiser erupted in flames, her magazines exploded, and the hulk rolled over and broke in half.

This small, brief action marked the first time an enemy warship had been sunk by air attack in World War II. (Japanese dive bombers had sunk the U.S. gunboat *Panay* in December 1937, but she was a shallow-draft, 450-ton river craft and the United States was not at war with Japan.)

Two days after the *Ark Royal* attack, the *Furious* sent off her 18 torpedo-armed Swordfish to strike German ships in the Norwegian port of Trondheim. The water was too shallow for torpedo attack, and the three German destroyers in port escaped. That same day the *Furious* launched a second strike, this time with the Swordfish each carrying four 250 lb (113 kg) bombs and four 20-pounders (9 kg bombs). Bad weather hampered the attackers, forcing some planes to turn back, and those that did get through were unable to inflict any damage.

Planes from the *Ark Royal* and *Furious* did damage a number of German merchant ships. These attacks cost the British several aircraft lost to anti-aircraft fire and to operational accidents—losses that were critical in view of their small aircraft capacities.

Despite these and other efforts by the British fleet, the German assault was a success. The carriers were then employed in withdrawal of the British forces that had been landed in Norway. The *Ark Royal* and *Glorious* flew aboard RAF Hurricane and Gladiator fighters, their pilots without carrier experience and their planes without arresting hooks.

After taking on board the fighters needed for the defense of Britain, the two carriers and accompanying escort ships set separate courses for Britain along with several merchant ships. Because of low fuel, the *Glorious* and a pair of destroyers took a more direct, and more dangerous, route home. On the afternoon of June 8 ship masts were seen on the horizon. The *Glorious* did not have all of her boilers ready while the wind direction as well as the exhaustion of her pilots prevented reconnaissance flights from being flown.

The German battle cruisers *Gneisenau* and *Scharnhorst*, each mounting nine 11 in (28 cm) guns, were able to take the carrier under fire before she could escape. Her two accompanying destroyers made valiant attacks. But salvo after salvo crashed into the *Glorious*, and at 5:20 p.m. the order was given to abandon ship. All three British ships were sunk, with one destroyer having scored a single torpedo hit on one of the German warships. One survivor of a destroyer was rescued by the Germans, while three days later a Norwegian ship rescued 38 survivors, and a German seaplane found another seven. A total of 1,515 British sailors and airmen died in this second loss of an aircraft carrier in combat.

Meanwhile, France and the Low Countries were invaded by German troops, and with the fall of France only a week away, on June 10, 1940, Italy declared war on Britain and France. In June the Royal Navy had lost the *Glorious* (as well as several other warships). Most of the previously allied French fleet was interned and the large Italian fleet now arrayed against Britain. While the Italians had no carriers or naval air arm, the Italian "boot" and the large island of Sicily provide numerous air bases that almost cut the Mediterranean in half. Transit through the "Med" was vital for the British. If forced to aban-

Fairey Swordfish Mk I
of No. 820 Squadron aboard the *Ark Royal* in 1940.

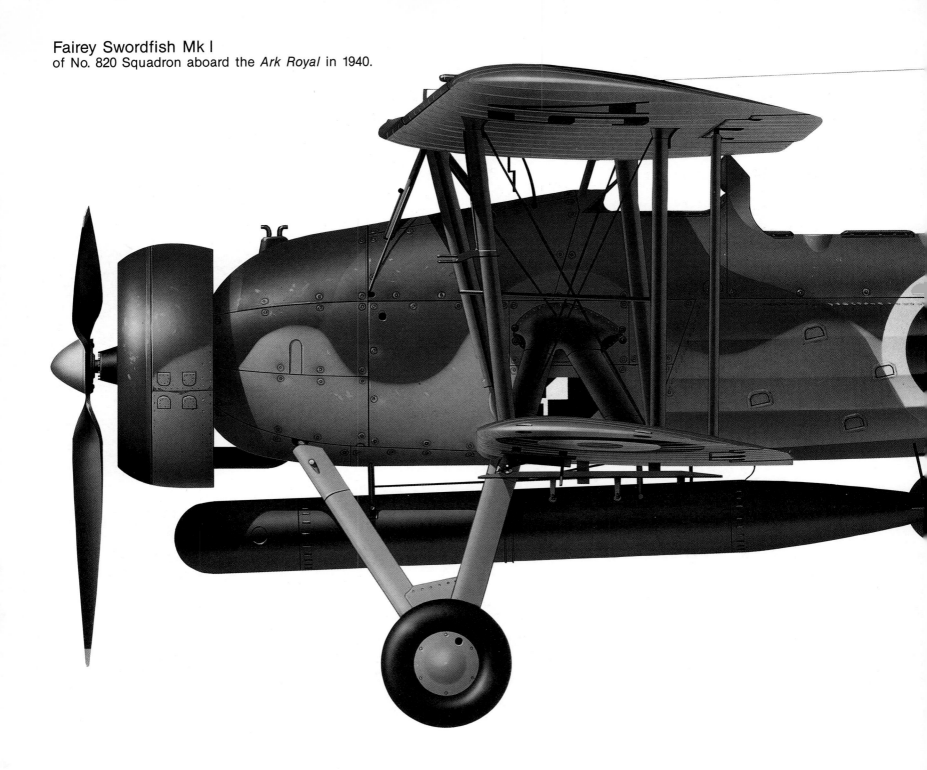

don the Mediterranean, British ships traveling between the Middle East and Britain or America would add weeks and thousands of miles to their transits.

Accordingly, on June 23 the carrier *Ark Royal* arrived at Gibraltar to keep watch on the large French warships that were at Oran (Mers-el-Kebir) in North Africa. Along with two battleships, a battle cruiser, a light cruiser, and four destroyers, the "Ark" formed Force H, an organization that would become famous in the long naval history of the Mediterranean.

The British government decided that the Frech warships at Oran—two battle cruisers, two old battleships, plus several destroyers and submarines—were considered an unacceptable threat to British operations in the Mediterranean. On July 3 the ships of Force H arrived off the port, and the captain of the *Ark Royal*, formerly British naval attaché in Paris, went ashore to negotiate with the French admirals.

Three alternatives were presented to the French: sail in company with the British warships and fight the Germans (as some other French ships had); sail to a British port with reduced

crews and have the ships laid up for the remainder of the war; or sail the ships to the West Indies or the United States where they could be laid up for the duration. But in no event could they remain ready for action in a French-controlled port.

The French admirals refused and announced that they would defend their ships. There was no alternative for Force H but to take action. First the *Ark Royal*'s Swordfish laid small fields of magnetic mines to prevent the French ships from leaving port. Then, after another effort was communicated to the French, the British warships opened fire. In 15 minutes several of the French ships were sunk or damaged with more than a thousand French dead. During the brief battle, one battle cruiser and five large destroyers escaped to sea.

The French ships passed within a few miles of the *Ark Royal*, but the ships were shrouded in haze. The French ships took no action. The carrier flew off a Swordfish strike, but they inflicted no damage, and the French warships safely reached the French port of Toulon. Although French shore-based aircraft attacked the Force H ships during the day, they inflicted no

Power unit
Bristol Pegasus IIIM3 nine-cylinder air-cooled engine
: 775 hp at sea level
  690 hp at 3,500 ft (1,070 m)
Dimensions
Span: 45 ft 6 in (13.87 m)
Span folded: 17 ft 3 in (5.26 m)
Length, tail up: 36 ft 4 in (11.07 m)
Height, tail up: 13 ft 5¾ in (4.11 m)
Wing area: 607 sq ft (56.4 m²)
Weights
Empty: 4,700 lb (2,130 kg)
Gross: 8,100 lb (3,670 kg)

Performance (at 8,700 lb/3,950 kg)
Max speed: 139 mph (224 km/h) at 4,750 ft (1,450 m)
Cruising speed: 104 mph (167 km/h) at 5,000 ft (1,520 m)
Time to climb to 5,000 ft (1,520 m): 10 min
Range with a 1,610 lb (730 kg) torpedo: 546 mls (879 km)
Range with a 69 lmp gal (314 ltr) drop tank: 1,030 mls (1,660 km)
Armament
Torpedo: 1 × 1,610 lb (730 kg)
Bombs: 1 × 1,500 lb (680 kg) or 3 × 500 lb (227 kg)
Fixed forward-firing: 1 × 0.303 in (7.7 mm) Vickers machine gun
Flexible mounted aft-firing: 1 × 0.303 in (7.7 m) Lewis machine gun
Crew
2 or 3

damage other than one French fighter shooting down a Skua fighter, but in turn being destroyed. Subsequently the *Ark Royal* flew another strike at Oran and inflicted more damage on the remaining, already damaged battle cruiser. (A Swordfish torpedo struck a tug loaded with depth charges that was alongside a battle cruiser; there was a violent explosion that ripped a hole 60 ft /18 m in the side of the warship.)

The French ships at the Egyptian port of Alexandria were put under British control without bloodshed. On the Western coast of Africa, at Dakar, the captain of the new French battleship *Richelieu* refused all British terms. Six torpedo planes from the *Hermes* attacked with torpedoes, one of which hit and inflicted some damage to the warship.

At Martinique in the West Indies the lone French carrier *Bearn* was preparing to return to France with American-built fighters for the French air force. With the fall of France the planes were unloaded, and the carrier remained at anchor for the rest of the war.

With the potential of French naval interference in the Mediterranean ended, Force H and the British Mediterranean Fleet at Alexandria could commence action against the Italians. At Alexandria was the outdated carrier *Eagle*, four older battleships, and several lesser warships. The *Eagle* now operated 17

Swordfish plus three Gladiator fighters. But the 1,900 miles (3,520 km) separating Alexandria from Force H was a gauntlet of Italian air, surface, and submarine attacks.

Roughly halfway between "Gib" and "Alex" lay the small island of Malta. This British possession was only 58 miles (107 km) from Italian Sicily. The small island, which began the war with a few Swordfish and Gladiators, became a vital base for carrying the war to the Italians. And, because of that, it became an important point in the naval war in the Mediterranean.

The first major engagement between the British and Italian fleets occurred off Calabria, the "toe" of the Italian "boot" in early July 1940. The carrier *Eagle*, three battleships, and their screen was covering two convoys moving from Malta to Alexandria. At sea were an Italian force of two battleships with a heavy cruiser and destroyer force, also covering a convoy.

The surface clash was brief. An Italian battleship and heavy cruiser were damaged, and the action broken off. The British ships gave chase, and the *Eagle* flew off a Swordfish torpedo strike, but no further damage was inflicted. Significantly, the Italian Air Force bombed the British ships—and the *Italian* ships as well. They scored no hits but claimed several successes in the battle; the Italian foreign minister wrote that the aircraft had destroyed half of the British naval power in the Mediterranean Sea!

The first plane, a Fairey Flumar Mk I two-seat fighter, leaves the deck of HMS *Ark Royal*, followed by the rest, Flumars and Blackburn Skua dive-bombers. (Imperial War Museum)

At the other end of the Med, the *Ark Royal* carried out strikes against Italian facilities on the island of Sardinia. There followed a long series of carrier operations in the Mediterranean as Force H provided carrier cover to convoys sailing from Gibraltar to Malta or through to Alexandria. In August the new carrier *Illustrious* joined Force H. On her decks were the familiar Swordfish plus Fulmar fighters, the Royal Navy's first modern figher, fitted with an armament of eight .303-caliber (7.7 mm) guns although its top speed was only 256 mph (412 km/h). Also important, the *Illustrious* had an armored flight deck.

With her arrival the *Ark Royal* could return to England for much-need repairs and maintenance. With the new *Illustrious* in the Med the decision was made to undertake the first major carrier strike operation in history: the attack against Taranto. Reconnaissance flights indicated that all six of Italy's battleships were in the port. A strike was planned using Swordfish from the *Eagle* and *Illustrious*. At the last moment, however, damage from previous near misses by Italian bombs caused the *Eagle* to remain in Alexandria. Five of her Swordfish were shifted to the *Illustrious*, and the fleet went to sea.

Could a lone carrier with obsolete aircraft inflict significant damage on six battleships, even resting at anchor? Late on the evening of November 11, 1940, the *Illustrious* flew off 12 Swordfish armed with bombs and torpedoes. Fifty minutes later the second wave of nine more Swordfish took to the skies, also with bombs and torpedoes. One plane lost its auxiliary fuel tank, forcing it to return to the carrier. The remaining 20 planes and their 40 crewmen flew on through the night.

They took the Italians by surprise. The lead planes had flares and bombs. Although the Italians were quick to respond with anti-aircraft fire, through the flare-lit sky the Swordfish attacked. When the raid was over the new 35,000-ton battleship *Littorio* had been hit by three torpedoes and beached to prevent sinking; the 26,622-ton battleship *Conte de Cavour* had sunk after a single torpedo hit, and her sister ship *Caio Duilio*, also hit by one torpedo, had been beached. A cruiser and a destroyer were damaged by bombs.

Half of the Italian battle fleet was out of the war for at least four months. (One battleship was never repaired.) The cost to the British was two Swordfish lost, with one crew dead and the other captured. The only Italian bombers to approach the *Illustrious* force—after the attack—jettisoned their bombs and fled. British convoys to Malta and Greece sailing at the same time as the Taranto raid got through safely. The aircraft carrier had again proven that, under the right circumstances, it could inflict heavy damage on enemy ships.

The *Ark Royal* returned to Gibraltar in November and the running of important convoys to and from Malta and Alexandria continued. In late November, as Force H was escorting a convoy, the Italian fleet came out to do battle with two battleships and lesser warships. After closing to do battle, the Italians broke away from the superior British battleship force. The *Ark Royal* flew off 11 Swordfish with torpedoes to attack and slow the Italian battleships. However, armed with torpedoes the Swordfish could fly about 90 mph (145 km/h). There was a headwind and the Italian ships were steaming away at some 30 knots. The Swordfish closing rate was less than 50 mph (80 km/h). The Swordfish were finally able to overtake their quarry and began their low torpedo runs. All 11 "fish" were launched at the battleships but scored no hits. The anti-aircraft fire was heavy, but no Swordfish were lost. A second flight—with nine torpedo planes and seven Skua dive bombers—also failed to inflict damage, and the Italian ships escaped.

The fateful year 1941 began with a complex British operation of moving convoys to Malta and to Greece, where British and Greek troops were attempting to stem the invasion by Hitler's legions. Force H with the *Ark Royal* performed its role in the operation and turned back toward Gibraltar. The Mediterranean Fleet with the *Illustrious* was about 85 miles (157 km) from Malta at noon on January 10. A pair of Italian bombers tried ineffectively to attack with torpedoes.

Suddenly, shipboard radar detected a large aircraft formation approaching the fleet. The *Illustrious* attempted to put up all 12 of her Fulmar fighters (whose rate of climb was *less* than the earlier Skua and Sea Gladiator fighters). The attackers came into view—40 to 50 German Ju87 Stukas—the gull-winged dive bombers that had devastated the battlefields of Europe. With split-second timing, the Stukas dived on the *Illustrious* at angles from 65 to 80 degrees.

The carrier vanished from sight as great cascades of water erupted from near misses of bombs. Six of the bombs

German PC500 (500 kg/1,102 lb) armor-piercing bomb

Used for anti-shipping. The bomb body is made of one-piece forged steel. The tail unit is constructed of sheet steel or magnesium alloy.

Length overall: 173.2 cm (68.2 in)
Body length: 107.4 cm (42.3 in)
Body diameter: 39.6 cm (15.6 in)
Weight of filling: 75 kg (165 lb)
Total Weight: 539 kg (1,188 lb)

1 Ring strut
2 Tail fins
3 Tail cone
4 Base plate
5 Fuze pocket
6 Body
7 Suspension lug
8 Explosive

smashed into the carrier. One was a 250 kg (551 lb) bomb, and the others were 500 kg (1,102 lb) bombs. In minutes the ship was out of control and wrapped in flames. No other carrier would ever absorb six direct hits and remain afloat.

The *Illustrious* did remain afloat, saved by her armored flight deck from being sent directly to the bottom of the Mediterranean. After three hours the ship was able to get up steam and limped toward Malta. More Italian and German planes attacked. A Stuka scored another hit with a 500 kg (1,102 lb) bomb.

Once within Malta's shipyard the repairs started immediately on the carrier while German planes continued to attack. The ordeal continued until darkness on January 23, when the *Illustrious* slipped out to sea and, at a speed of 20 knots, steamed toward Alexandria and safety. She reached port safely and then steamed south through the Suez Canal, around Africa, and across the Atlantic to an American shipyard where ten months of work were required to return her to full service. Air attacks had not sunk the *Illustrious*, but for the first time in his-

tory aircraft had left a carrier dead in the water and gasping for life.

Although there was now only one carrier in the Mediterranean, the Italian battle fleet was reluctant to give battle. The *Ark Royal* continued to cover convoys and was briefly directed into the Atlantic to search for the battle cruisers *Gneisenau* and *Scharnhorst*, which had earlier sunk the *Glorious*. A Fulmar fighter located the German ships, but its radio malfunctioned; the plane raced back to the carrier, and Swordfish were launched but could not find the ship.

Meanwhile, the carrier *Formidable* arrived at Alexandria. In addition to Fulmars and Swordfish, she carried the new Albacore torpedo plane. It was still a biplane but had an enclosed cockpit, a speed of 160 mph (260 km/h), and other performance advantages over the Swordfish. Both planes could carry an 18 in (45.7 cm), 1,610 lb (730 kg) torpedo, but where the Swordfish could alternatively load 1,500 lb (680 kg) of bombs, the newer plane could load 2,000 lb (910 kg).

The *Formidable*'s combat debut came in late March when the Mediterranean Fleet encountered three Italian groups at sea, one centered on a battleship and two cruiser forces. The first target of the *Illustrious* was the group with the battleship *Vittorio Veneto* and four destroyers. The dreadnought had escaped damage in the Taranto strike. Six Albacores attacked. No torpedoes hit. Strikes by Albacores, Swordfish, and land-based RAF bombers continued, and a Swordfish scored a hit that slowed the battleship. The two cruiser groups closed to protect her while the *Illustrious* sent off all available planes for a final strike—six Albacores and two Swordfish, with another pair of "Stringbags" flying from Crete.

Although damaged, the *Vittorio Veneto* evaded all torpedoes launched at her, but one "fish" struck and stopped the 10,000-ton cruiser *Pola*. Two other cruisers and four destroyers slowed to screen the damaged ship. That night the British main force came across them and in a brief engagement sank all three cruisers and two destroyers. Thus, five Italian warships had been sunk and a battleship damaged at the cost of one Swordfish shot down (the one that had scored the hit on the *Vittorio Veneto*) and its three-man crew. The victory was possible because of that single torpedo hit. This action—one hundred miles off Cape Matapan, Greece—was the world's first major fleet action since World War I and the first time that an aircraft carrier had participated in such an action.

In May 1941 the new carrier *Victorious* sailed from England with the main British fleet to seek out the German battleship *Bismarck* which, with a cruiser, had broken out into the Atlantic and, in a few salvos, sank the large battle cruiser *Hood* and damaged the new battleship *Prince of Wales*. One *Victorious* Swordfish scored a torpedo hit on the German battleship, but inflicted no damage on the heavily armored ship.

Force H with the *Ark Royal* was sent out into the Atlantic in an attempt to intercept the Germans before they reached the safety of a French port. On March 26 the "Ark" launched 10 search planes followed by 14 torpedo-armed Swordfish. The seas were rough, and at times the wind over the deck was 50 knots (26 m/sec).

After an hour's flight the Swordfish sighted a large ship on radar and began their attack. Only after 11 torpedoes were in the water did they realize that their target was a British cruiser! The ship—HMS *Sheffield*—evaded the deadly attack.

The *Ark Royal* heads for Malta with the convoy. (Imperial War Museum)

The *Ark Royal* recovered the planes, and at 7:10 p.m. she launched a strike of 15 Swordfish carrying torpedoes. This time they found the proper target and, despite the intensive anti-aircraft fire, launched against the 42,000-ton battleship. Two torpedoes hit. One struck the massive armored belt and inflicted no damage. The explosion of the second damaged the ship's propellers and jammed her rudders. This hit sealed the battleship's fate.

Her speed and maneuverability reduced, the *Bismarck* was easily caught by a British battle force and, after a severe pounding by guns and ship-launched torpedoes, slid beneath the waves.

In the eastern Mediterranean the Germans triumphed in Greece as the British desperately tried to evacuate their troops. Many were brought to the island of Crete, which lies a-stride the entrance to the Aegean Sea. In late May the Germans carried out a massive parachute assault on the island. The hard-pressed Mediterranean Fleet attempted to support the British forces on Crete. Again the Ju87 Stukas struck. This time their target was the *Formidable*. On May 26 she was attacked by 20 dive bombers which scored two hits with 500 kg (1,102 lb) bombs. Her armored deck saved her from serious damage, but she was withdrawn for repairs. The planes were from the same unit that had smashed the *Illustrious*. The next day the decision was made to evacuate Crete, and the island fell on June 1. (The *Formidable* also steamed to the United States for repairs and for an upgraded anti-aircraft battery.)

After the *Bismarck* episode, the exhausted pilots of the *Ark Royal* and the *Victorious* rested and assessed their loss-es. On June 13 they departed Gibraltar to screen a convoy to Malta. For the next few months they successfully operated in the western Med. Often they crarried RAF fighters that were flown into Malta, in addition to their naval aircraft, and the venerable *Furious* was also employed in this ferry role.

The carriers were regularly subjected to Italian and German air attacks, and periodically they were threatened by German U-boats. The *Ark Royal*'s good fortune ended on the afternoon of November 13, 1941. The U81 scored a single torpedo hit on the carrier. Only one man was killed in the carrier, but she soon lost power, and despite intensive damage control efforts, she continued to take on water and was lost.

With the loss of the *Ark Royal*—the third British carrier sunk in the war—the Royal Navy was without a carrier in the Mediterranean for the first time since Italy entered the war in June 1940. The shortage of carriers led the British to initiate conversions of merchant ships to aircraft carriers. The first was a former German merchant ship, converted and placed in service in June 1941 as HMS *Audacity*. No hangar deck was fitted, and she could embark only six aircraft, American-built F4F Wildcat fighters that were called Martlets by the British.

From September to December 1941 the 5,537 (gross)-ton *Audacity* proved a most useful convoy escort ship, her Martlets searching for submarines and also being able to chase away German reconnaissance planes that attempted to track convoys. On the night of December 21-22 the U751 scored a torpedo hit on the small flattop, and her brief career was at an end. Many more escort carriers would follow, and some would encounter enemy battle fleets—some at very close ranges.

Japanese on the Rampage

The Japanese Navy first flew combat operations from aircraft carriers in the war with China during the late 1930s. This experience, coupled with the large carrier building program and the high performance of the A6M Zero, gave the Japanese Navy a most effective carrier force. There were nine carriers in service by December 1941 with more than 400 aircraft embarked:

CV   *Akagi* (66 planes)
CV   *Kaga* (75 planes)
CV   *Hiryu* (54 planes)
CV   *Soryu* (54 planes)
CV   *Shokaku* (72 planes)
CV   *Zuikaku* (72 planes)
CVL *Zuiho* (27 planes)
CVL *Ryujo* (34 planes)
CVE *Hosho* (19 planes)

The 11,200-ton *Zuiho* was begun as a submarine tender but completed in 1940 as a light carrier. Her sister ship *Shoho*, which was completed in 1940 as a submarine tender, was taken in hand for a similar conversion and would be ready in early 1942. The six largest carriers were organized into the First Air Fleet, a more powerful concentration of air striking power than had ever before been assembled at sea by any navy.

The fall of France to German armies in June 1940 was followed by Japanese occupation of Indochina. The need for resources from the Dutch East Indies made it obvious that the Japanese would strike to the south, while the virtually undefended Philippine Islands, an American commonwealth that lay astride shipping routes between Japan and the East Indies, would also be a target as would British possessions in the Far East—Hong Kong and Malaya.

The major opposition to such Japanese thrusts would be the U.S. fleet, based since April 1940 at Pearl Harbor in the Hawaiian Islands. Realizing that the massive shipbuilding program under way in the United states would by 1943 make the U.S. fleet far superior to Japan's, Admiral Isoroku Yamamoto, Commander in Chief of the Japanese Combined Fleet, planned an attack against the fleet at Pearl Harbor at the start of hostilities. This attack was carefully planned and "gamed," and although perhaps two of six carriers in the attack were expected to be lost, the opportunity to delay the U.S. fleet from sailing westward for perhaps six months seemed an achieveable objective.

The U.S. fleet was placed at Pearl Harbor by President Franklin D. Roosevelt as a deterrent to Japanese aggression in the Pacific. But at the same time Roosevelt was transferring ships to the Atlantic, to provide short-of-war support for Great Britain. By December 1941 there were but three U.S. carriers in the Pacific:

CV-2 *Lexington* (72 planes)
CV-3 *Saratoga* (72 planes)
CV-6 *Enterprise* (72 planes)

Thus, the Japanese fleet considerably outnumbered the U.S. carrier forces in the Pacific as well as in every other major warship category. (Even including available British and Dutch ships, the Japanese were superior in every ship type except for light cruisers.)

The four other U.S. large carriers, plus escort carrier *Long Island* (at the time AVG-1, later CVE-1), newly converted from a merchant ship, were in the Atlantic:

CV-4 *Ranger* (72 planes)
CV-5 *Yorktown* (72 planes)
CV-7 *Wasp* (72 planes)
CV-8 *Hornet* (69 planes)
CVE-1 *Long Island* (20 planes)

The pioneer U.S. carrier *Langley* had been converted in 1937 to a seaplane tender. Her flight deck was cut back preventing her from operating carrier-type aircraft.

The crescendo of events in the Pacific let to the sailing of the Japanese striking force from Hitokappu Bay in the bleak Kuril Islands on November 26, 1941. In addition to the six carriers of the First Air Fleet, the force consisted of two battleships, two heavy cruisers, a light cruiser, nine destroyers, and eight oilers. A total of 30 submarines were also involved in the operation. Including fighters to be held for defense of the task force, the six carriers had 389 aircraft on their decks.

Travelling on a northerly course to avoid merchant ships, the striking force encountered heavy seas that broke away fuel lines and washed sailors overboard. En route the message to carry out the attack was received. Eight in the morning on Sunday, December 7, was the moment for the first bombs to strike.

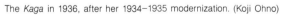
The *Kaga* in 1936, after her 1934–1935 modernization. (Koji Ohno)

At Pearl Harbor that Sunday there were eight U.S. battleships, 21 cruisers, 41 destroyer-type ships, and five submarines, plus lesser ships. The U.S. carriers would escape the attack: the *Enterprise* and *Lexington* were at sea, carrying Marine aircraft to the island bases of Wake and Midway, respectively, and the *Saratoga* was at San Diego, California.

At 6 p.m. on December 7, from a position 190 miles (350 km) NNE of the island of Oahu, the Japanese carriers began to launch aircraft. There were 43 Zero fighters and 140 D3A Val and B5N Kate bombers in the first wave. The fighters and dive bombers were to strike the airfields to destroy U.S. fighters and other aircraft. Of the Kates, 40 were armed with torpedoes and the other 49 carried 800 kg (1,764 lb) bombs, adopted from 16 in (40.6 cm) armor-piercing shells, to attack the fleet. The torpedoes were especially modified to permit their use in the shallow waters of Pearl Harbor—which American admirals had thought provided protection from aerial torpedo attack.

While the first strike was in flight, a second wave was launched: 35 Zeroes, 78 Val dive bombers, and 54 Kates, a total of 167 planes. These Kates had bombs to strike airfields while the Vals were each armed with 250 kg (551 lb) bombs to attack ships. Each wave was a larger air strike than had ever before been flown in a naval engagement.

At 7: 55 a.m. the first Japanese bomb struck the naval air station on Ford Island in the center of Pearl Harbor. The Americans were taken by complete surprise. During the next two hours the attackers sank four battleships and damaged the four others; sank three destroyers and a minelayer; damaged several other ships; and destroyed 188 Navy and Army aircraft. Their bombs, torpedoes, and bullets killed 2,335 Americans.

The cost to the Japanese was 29 aircraft that were lost in combat and operationally with 55 fliers. A small price to pay for what one Japanese pilot described as "Pearl Harbor [is] in flame and smoke, gasping helplessy...." (Also lost would be one large submarine and the five midget craft that participated in the attack; they sank no ships.)

The air attack had failed to significantly damage the shipyard facilities and the oil storage tanks. The strike leaders sought permission to make another strike, but the task force commander, pleased with the results and small losses, and fearing an attack from the undetected U.S. carriers, refused and ordered a withdrawal. Had the base facilities been attacked the surviving U.S. fleet would have had to retreat to the West Coast, delaying American operations against the Japanese by several months.

Nakajima Type 97 Model 3 (Mk 12) carrier-based torpedo-bomber (Kate) from the *Zuikaku* over burning Pearl Harbor on December 7, 1941. (Kiyokuma Okajima)

The capsized *Oklahoma* and damaged battleships at Pearl Harbor after Japanese surprise attack. (National Archives)

The opening blow against the U.S. fleet was devastating for the Americans. It could have been much worse. Had the U.S. carriers been at Pearl Harbor they, too, would surely have been sunk. Or, if the battle fleet had been at sea the results would undoubtedly been similar. What if the Japanese carrier force had encountered two or even three U.S. carriers at sea? While the battle would have depended in large part on which side sighted the other first and other tactical factors, the larger number of Japanese aircraft and their pilots' combat experience from China would probably have seen an overwhelming Japanese victory. But the first carrier-versus-carrier battle was five months away.

Returning from the Pearl Harbor attack, two of the Japanese carriers sent bombers against the small U.S. outpost of Wake Island to support the Japanese landings. An American task force, centered on the carrier *Saratoga* and a seaplane tender that was steaming to reinforce (or if need be evacuate) Wake, was withdrawn after the *Shokaku* and *Zuikaku* bombed Wake for fear that the American ships were steaming into a trap. (The Japanese had no knowledge of the approaching U.S. ships, which came within 425 miles/787 km of Wake before turning back.) Wake surrendered to the Japanese on December 22.

The striking force returned to Japan amid victory celebrations. Simultaneous with the carrier attack on Pearl Harbor, Japanese forces initiated assaults against Wake, the Philippines, and Malaya, followed by the conquest of New Britain, the Dutch East Indies, and Burma. Two days after the Pearl Harbor raid, on December 9, the British task force at Singapore steamed northward to attack Japanese transports that were landing troops on the coast of Malaya.

The British force consisted of the new battleship *Prince of Wales* and the older but still-powerful battle cruiser *Repulse*, plus four destroyers. There was no carrier with the force. Except for the small, obsolete *Hermes* in the Indian Ocean, there was no Allied carrier between Pearl Harbor and Suez. Land-based fighters from Singapore were assigned to support the British capital ships, but they were a significant distance away, under RAF control, and there were communications problems.

Thus, on the morning of December 10 the *Prince of Wales* and *Repulse* and their four destroyers were dependent upon their own weapons for defense. Land-based Japanese naval aircraft from Indochina were searching the area—11 reconnaissance planes, 52 twin-engine bombers armed with torpedoes, and another 34 bombers with bombs. First they attacked a destroyer detached from the main force, and then the capital ships felt the weight of the Japanese attack. The attack began shortly after 11 a.m. At 12:33 the *Repulse* keeled over and sank, struck by one 250 kg (551 lb) bomb and five torpedoes. The *Prince of Wales* survived another 47 minutes. One or two 500 kg (1,102 lb) bombs and six torpedoes caused her to turn turtle and sink. The Japanese lost three aircraft, each with a seven man crew, in the attack. The British lost two capital ships and 840 men, including the admiral commanding. (The destroyers rescued the other crewmen.)

The sinking of the *Prince of Wales* and *Repulse* had importance far beyond their specific loss. At Taranto and Pearl Harbor the targets were battleships lying at anchor, internal compartments open, unable to get under way, and with their guns unmanned. Off the coast of Malaya on December 10 the targets were maneuvering at high speed, closed up for action, and putting up heavy anti-aircraft fire. Still, with minimal losses, the Japanese Navy had demonstrated that warships under all conditions were vulnerable to aerial attack.

While the six large carriers of the First Air Fleet were carrying out the Pearl Harbor strike, the light carrier *Ryujo* provided air support for the invasion of the Philippines (most of the Japanese planes in that assault flew from the island of Formosa). The First Air Fleet, less the two ships detached to bomb Wake, arrived in Japan on December 23. After replenishing, on January 9 the *Akagi*, *Kaga*, *Shokaku*, and *Zuikaku* and their screen steamed south for combat. On the 20th their planes struck the British base at Rabaul on New Britain and afterwards Lae and Salamaua on New Guinea. The *Hiryu* and *Soryu* then entered the air, and strikes were continued against Allied bases, including northern Australia. There was no serious opposition to the Japanese carrier pilots, and there were few Allied surface ships for them to attack. The pioneer U.S. carrier *Langley*, serv-

The *Hermes*'s last moments on April 9, 1942. (Koji Ohno)

ing as an aircraft transport taking P-40 fighters to Java, was sunk on February 23 by land-based Japanese planes.

In late March five carriers of the First Air Fleet steamed into the Indian Ocean, the *Kaga* having been sent back to Japan for repairs. The British now had in the Indian Ocean the new carriers *Formidable* and *Indomitable*, the venerable *Hermes*, several battleships, and a number of cruisers and destroyers. There were also some 300 land-based RAF and naval aircarft on Ceylon and Indian airfields along the Bay of Bengal.

When the Japanese carrier force was sighted approaching Ceylon on April 4, the British battle fleet was too faraway to engage in action—which would probably have been disastrous for the under-strength British carrier squadrons. On April 5 the Japanese struck facilities in Colombo with 128 aircraft. The Japanese concentrated on the naval facilities and only one destroyer and one merchant ship were sunk. While the Colombo raid was in progress, 53 Val dive bombers found two British heavy cruisers and, in 19 minutes, every one of their bombs scored a hit or near miss, except one bomb that failed to release. Four hundred twenty-five British officers and enlisted men died with those two ships. There were no Japanese losses (the Colombo strike cost seven carrier planes).

There were more strikes against the shore, and on April 9 the Japanese sighted the *Hermes* off the coast of Trincomalee. Eighty-five Val dive bombers fell on the carrier, which was without defensive fighter cover. In a few minutes the *Hermes* and an Australian destroyer with her were sunk. Another 315 British and Australian sailors died. The *Hermes*—the first ship begun as an aircraft carrier—had the distinction of being the first aircraft carrier to be sunk by planes from another carrier.

En route back to their carriers the Japanese planes sank several smaller British ships. And, while the *Hermes* was being sunk, nine British land-based bombers attacked the carrier *Akagi*. Not since the war began four months before had a bomb fallen on a Japanese carrier. There was no damage inflicted, and five British planes were shot down. In all, the Japanese lost ten planes on April 9.

The First Air Fleet withdrew from the Indian Ocean. The smaller carrier *Ryujo* and a cruiser-destroyer force entered the Bay of Bengal on an anti-shipping raid where they sank 23 merchant ships. Afterwards, Japanese submarines continued to attack British merchant ships in the area.

During this period the U.S. Pacific Fleet undertook a series of limited operations to keep the shipping routes to Australia open and to carry out limited raids against Japanese forces. There could be no attempt to reinforce the Philippines with the limited forces available—four large carriers and attendant cruisers and destroyers. After Pearl Harbor the *Yorktown* had quickly transited through the Panama Canal into the Pacific, to join the *Lexington*, *Saratoga*, and *Enterprise*. But the "Sara" was struck by a torpedo from the Japanese submarine I-16 while south of Hawaii; the carrier returned to Pearl Harbor and then steamed to the U.S. West Coast where she was out of service for five months being repaired and having her anti-aircraft batteries increased.

The first U.S. carrier strike of the war was to be against Wake. A force built around the *Lexington* sortied from Pearl Harbor, but when a Japanese submarine sank the only available fleet oiler the raid was called off. Next the *Yorktown* and *Enterprise* sailed westward to attack Japanese-held atolls in the Marshall Islands. With little opposition from land-based aircraft, the carrier planes shot up Japanese aircraft and small merchant ships and bombed installations. As important as the damage inflicted, the raids were an invaluable training ground for the pilots and crews of the carriers and their F4F Wildcat fighters, SBD Dauntless dive bombers, and TBD Devastator torpedo planes.

The next U.S. carrier target was to be Rabaul, but the approaching *Lexington* force was sighted, and the carrier withdrew in the midst of significant air attacks. The carriers continued these strikes, hitting Wake, Marcus, and Salamaua on New Guinea. A more dramatic—and if possible effective—carrier strike was needed to slow Japanese plans and to boost American morale, badly shattered by the Japanese successes of the past four months.

Early in the war U.S. naval officers had conceived a raid against Japan by U.S. Army bombers launched from a Navy carrier. A pair of twin-engine B-25B bombers, with a wingspan of 67 ft 7 in (20.6 m) and weighing some 29,000 lb

Nakajima Type 97 Model 1 (Mk 11)
carrier-based torpedo-bomber
(B5N1, Allied code name: Kate)
of the *Hiryu Kogekiki-Tai* (Attacker Unit) in 1940.

Power unit
Nakajima *Hikari* Mk 3 9-cylinder air-cooled engine
: 830 hp for take-off
 710 hp at 2,600 m (8,530 ft)
Dimensions
Span: 15.518 m (50 ft 11 in)
Span folded: 7.30 m (23 ft 11⁷/₁₆ in)
Length, tail up: 10.30 m (33 ft 9¹/₂ in)
Height, tail up: 3.815 m (12 ft 6³/₁₆ in)
Wing area: 37.69 m² (405.72 sq ft)
Weights
Empty: 2,099 kg (4,627 lb)
Normal gross: 3,700 kg (8,160 lb)
Performance
Max speed: 369 km/h (229 mph) at 2,000 m (6,560 ft)
Cruising speed: 256 km/h (158 mph) at 2,000 m (6,560 ft)
Time to climb to 3,000 m (9,840 ft): 7 min 50 sec
Normal range: 1,224 km (761 mls)
Overloaded range: 2,259 km (1,404 mls)
Armament
Torpedo: 1 × 800 kg (1,764 lb)
Bombs: 1 × 800 kg (1,764 lb) or 2 × 250 kg (551 lb)
       or 6 × 60 kg (132 lb)
Flexible mounted aft-firing: 1 × 7.7 mm (0.303 in)
               Type *Ru* (Lewis) machine gun

Crew
3

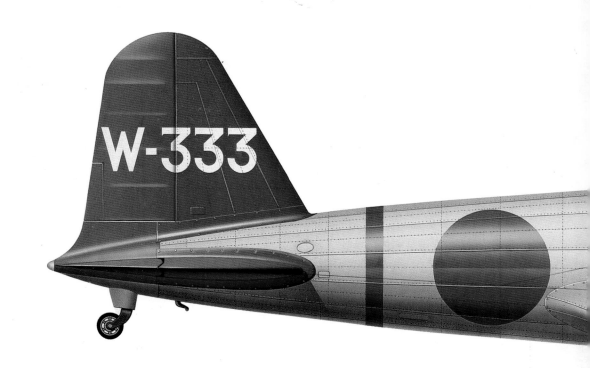

Scale ¹/₂₈

Aichi Type 99 Mk 11 carrier-based dive-bombers (D3A1/Val) from the *Zuikaku* attack the *Yorktown* (CV-5) on May 8, 1942, during the Battle of the Coral Sea. The *Lexington* (CV-2), attacked by Type 99 bombers from the *Shokaku,* is seen on the right of the cutaway.

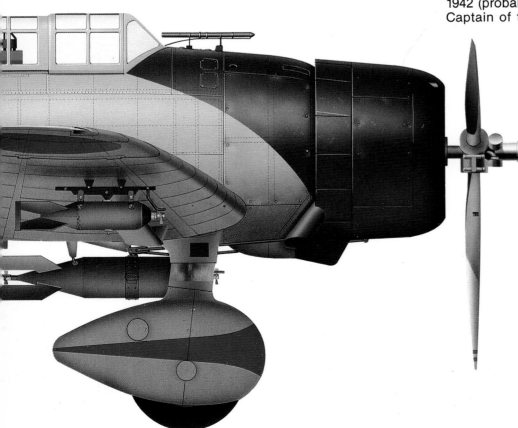

Aichi Type 99 Mk 11
carrier-based dive-bomber (D3A1, Allied code name: Val)
of the *Shokaku Bakugekiki-Tai* (Dive-bomber Unit) in January
1942 (probably flown by Lt Commander Kakuichi Takahashi,
Captain of the *Shokaku* Flying Group).

Power unit
Mitsubishi *Kinsei* Mk 44 14-cylinder air-cooled engine
: 1,000 hp for take-off
 990 hp at 2,800 m (9,190 ft)
Dimensions
Span: 14.36 m (47 ft 1³/₈ in)
Span folded: 10.93 m (35 ft 10⁵/₁₆ in)
Length, tail up: 10.185 m (33 ft 5 in)
Height, tail up: 3.90 m (12 ft 9⁹/₁₆ in)
Wing area: 34.9 m² (375.7 sq ft)
Weights
Empty: 2,390 kg (5,270 lb)
Normal gross: 3,650 kg (8,050 lb)
Performance
Max speed: 382 km/h (237 mph) at 2,320 m (7,610 ft)
Cruising speed: 296 km/h (184 mph) at 3,000 m (9,840 ft)
Time to climb to 3,000 m (9,840 ft): 6 min 27 sec
Normal range: 919 km (571 mls)
 Range with an auxiliary fuel tank: 1,472 km (915 mls)
Armament
Bombs: 1 × 250 kg (551 lb) and 2 × 60 kg (132 lb)
Fixed forward-firing: 2 × 7.7 mm (0.303 in)
                        Type 97 machine guns
Flexible mounted aft-firing: 1 × 7.7 mm (0.303 in)
                              Type 92 machine gun

Crew
2

Douglas SBD-3 Dauntless
of VB-6 on the USS *Enterprise* (CV-6) on June 4, 1942, during the Battle of Midway.

Power unit
Wright R-1820-52 14-cylinder air-cooled engine
: 1,000 hp for take-off
800 hp at 16,000 ft (4,880 m)
Dimensions
Span: 41 ft 6¹/₈ in (12.652 m)
Length, tail up: 32 ft 8 in (9.96 m)
Height, tail up: 13 ft 7 in (4.14 m)
Wing area: 323 sq ft (30.08 m²)
Weights
Empty: 6,345 lb (2,878 kg)
Gross: 9,407 lb (4,267 kg)
Performance
Max speed: 250 mph (402 km/h) at 16,000 ft (4,880 m)
Cruising speed: 152 mph (245 km/h)
Rate of climb: 1,190 ft (363 m)/min
Time to climb to 10,000 ft (3,050 m): 9 min
Range with a 1,000 lb (454 kg) bomb: 1,205 mls (1,940 km)
Range as scout: 1,415 mls (2,280 km)
Armament
Bombs: 1 × 1,000 lb (454 kg) and 2 × 100 lb (45 kg)
Fixed forward-firing: 2 × 0.50 in (12.7 mm) Browning M2 machine guns
Flexible mounted aft-firing: 2 × 0.30 in (7.62 mm) Browning M2 (M1919A2) machine guns
Crew

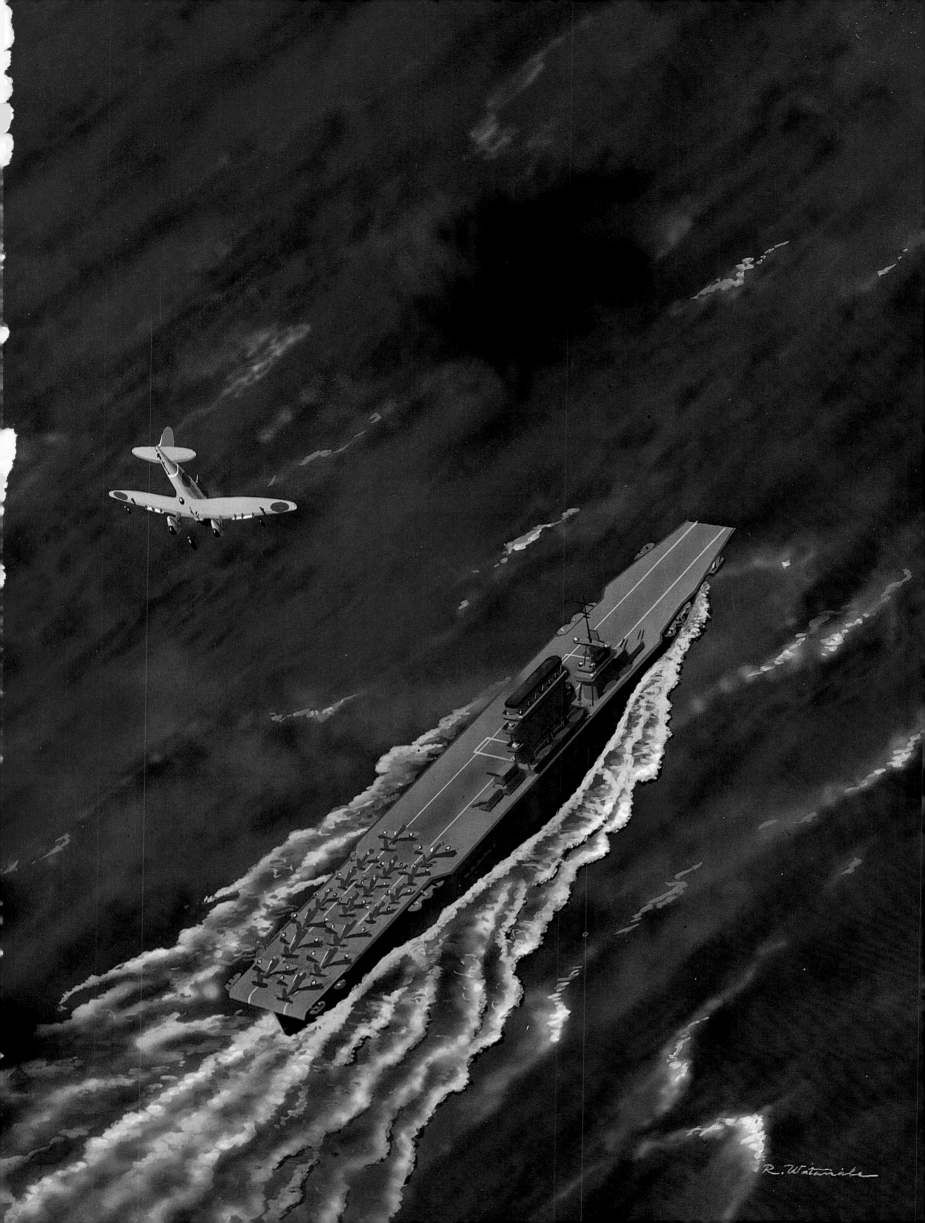

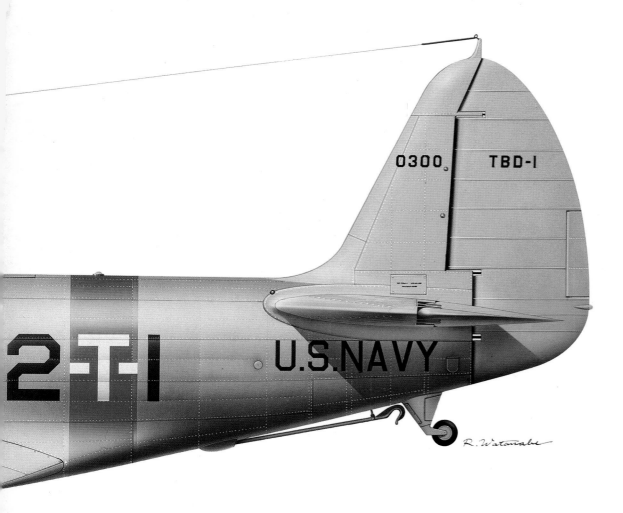

Douglas TBD-1 Devastator
flown by Squadron commander of VT-2
on the USS *Lexington* (CV-2) in 1939.

Power unit
Pratt & Whitney R-1830-64 14-cylinder air-cooled engine
: 900 hp for take-off
850 hp at 8,000 ft (2,440 m)
Dimensions
Span: 50 ft 0 in (15.24 m)
Span folded: 25 ft 8 in (7.82 m)
Length, tail up: 35 ft 0 in (10.67 m)
Height, tail up: 15 ft 1 in (4.60 m)
Wing area: 422 sq ft (39.2 m²)
Weights
Empty: 6,182 lb (2,804 kg)
Gross: 9,862 lb (4,473 kg)
Performance
Max speed: 206 mph (332 km/h) at 8,000 ft (2,440 m)
Cruising speed: 128 mph (206 km/h)
Rate of climb: 720 ft (219 m)/min
Range with a torpedo: 435 mls (700 km)
Range with a 1,000 lb (454 kg) bomb: 716 mls (1,152 km)
Armament
Torpedo: 1 × 1,700 lb (771 kg)
Bomb: 1 × 1,000 lb (454 kg)
Fixed forward-firing: 1 × 0.50 in (12.7 mm) Browning M2
     or 0.30 in (7.62 mm) Browning M2
     (M1919A2) machine gun
Flexible mounted aft-firing: 1 × 0.30 in (7.62 mm)
       Browning M2 (M1919A2)
       machine gun

Crew
3

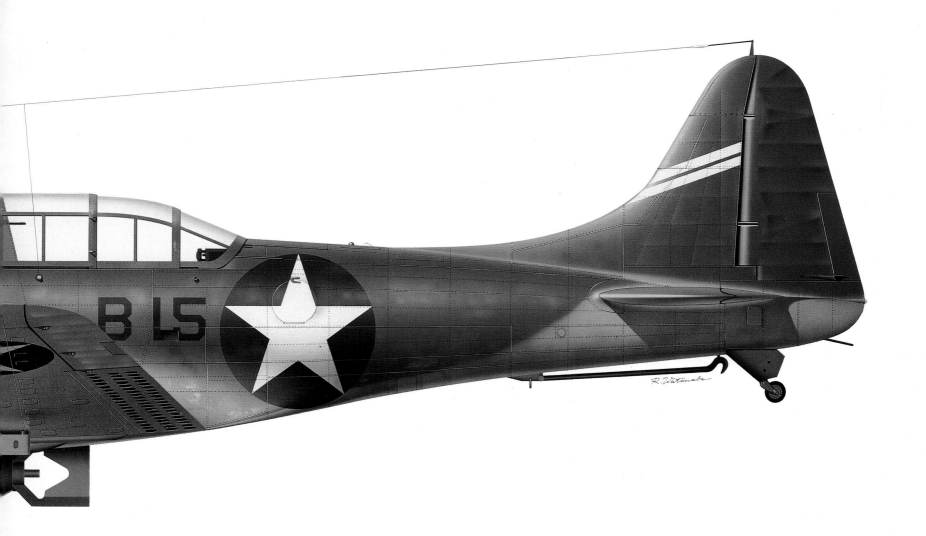

Scale 1/28

U.S. Army B-25B is launched from the *Hornet* in rough weather on April 18, 1942. (National Archives)

(13,150 kg), were loaded on board the *Hornet* by crane. She successfully flew them off during a test run in the Atlantic. The carrier then sped south, transited the Panama Canal, and arrived at San Francisco to load 16 of the B-25B Mitchell bombers.

The *Hornet* headed west for an at-sea rendezvous with the *Enterprise*, which had her normal carrier air squadrons embarked. The two carriers, with accompanying cruisers, destroyers, and oilers continued westward. The plan was to launch the bombers when 500 miles (930 km) from Japan. They would strike various military targets in Tokyo and other cities, and then fly on to land in China where they would join other U.S. air forces fighting the Japanese.

Early on April 18 radar in the U.S. ships sighted several small ships. The carriers were still some 700 miles (1,300 km) from Japan. A change in course was ordered, but more of the picket boats were sighted. They were taken under fire, but a warning had been sent to Japan. The U.S. carriers increased speed and made a run toward Japan; at 8 a.m. on April 18 the bombers, led by Lieutenant Colonel James (Jimmy) Doolittle, began to take off from the *Hornet*. They were 650 miles (1,200 km) from the Japanese coast and overloaded as additional fuel had been taken on.

Their raid caught Japan by surprise, as the U.S. carriers were expected to come much closer before launching a strike because of the limited range of the carrier aircraft they were thought to have. the B-25s raced in low, each releasing a 500 lb (227 kg) bomb and an incendiary cluster. Some damage was inflicted, but the importance of the raid was mainly psychological—on both Japan and the United States.

After bombing Japan all of the 16 planes ran out of fuel and crashed in China, except for one that came down in Siberia. Of their 75 crewmen, five died accidently and ten were captured by the Japanese. In violation of international law, the Japanese tried the ten by military court—three were shot and one other died in prison. Of the others, including five captured by the Soviets, all were returned to the United States. Nine men died in a carrier raid that was historic and which accelerated Japanese planning for the Midway operation and gave American a tremendous boost in morale.

The First Air Fleet, having returned from the Indian Ocean foray, replenished in Japan in preparation of the coming Midway operation. The *Shokaku* and *Zuikaku*, however, were sent south to serve as a backup force for the Japanese assault on Port Moresby, New Guinea. This base would put Japanese land-based aircraft within range of Australia. The newly converted light carrier *Shoho*, with 7 Zeros, 5 old A5M Claude fighters, and 10 Kate torpedo planes, would provide air cover for the assault force.

The U.S. Navy, helped by decoding Japanese radio transmissions, correctly assumed the target of the Japanese assault, and the U.S. carriers *Lexington* and *Yorktown* steamed toward the Coral Sea to intercept the Japanese invasion force. On their decks were 143 aircraft. The two Japanese large carriers had 126 planes on board, the *Shoho* had 20, and there were 120 land-based aircraft on Rabaul that could reach the combat area.

The U.S. commander was timid, knowing that he had much of the available U.S. naval power at risk; the Japanese commander was confident and unaware of the presence of the U.S. carriers. The carrier battle of the Coral Sea began on the morning of May 7 when a Japanese reconnaissance plane reported a U.S. carrier and cruiser some 200 miles (370 km) south of the *Shokaku* and *Zuikaku*. A strike was immediately launched. While the planes were en route, there was another report of an American carrier and ten other ships some 280 miles (520 km) from the Japanese carriers.

The first strike found only a U. S. oiler and destroyer, which had been incorrectly reported. The 78 Japanese planes quickly sank the U.S. ships, with only one plane lost. But the American force made the same mistake, flying off a large strike against what were reported as two carriers although they were in fact only a couple of old light cruisers. The U.S. aircraft—18 fighters, 53 dive bombers, and 22 torpedo planes—came across the hapless *Shoho*. The 93 attacking planes smothered the small Japanese carrier. Thirteen bombs and seven torpedoes hit the ship, and moments later a U.S. pilot radioed, "Scratch one flat-top," as the *Shoho* slipped beneath the waves. Some 600 of her crew of 800 were killed. Three U.S. planes were lost in the attack.

A Douglas SBD-3 Dauntless in the foreground and Douglas TBD-1 Devastators queue for takeoff from the fleet carrier (the *Enterprise*) in May 1942. (National Archives)

Meanwhile, the Japanese carrier commander launched another strike to attack the second U.S. group of ships—which were in fact the carriers *Lexington* and *Saratoga*. Twelve dive bombers and 15 torpedo planes were launched, but in the deteriorating weather conditions they could not locate the U.S. ships; after jettisoning their weapons and turning back, they came across the U.S. ships, and eight were shot down; another one plunged into the sea while trying to land on board the Japanese ships. (Reportedly, in the darkness a couple almost landed on board the carrier *Yorktown*!)

On the morning of May 8 the two Japanese carriers flew off scout planes followed by a strike of 69 aircraft. These planes found the U.S. carriers, and the 33 Val dive bombers and 18 torpedo-armed Kates pushed home their attacks. The *Yorktown* took only one hit, a 250 kg (551 lb) bomb, but it inflicted

serious damage to the ship. The larger *Lexington* received more attention and was struck by two torpedoes and five bombs. The bombs did little damage, and the list caused by the torpedoes was soon corrected.

Suddenly, there was a gigantic internal explosion aboard the *Lexington*. The torpedo hits had caused minor damage to the ship's gasoline storage tanks, and the escaping vapors had been ignited by an electric generator. Fires spread rapidly and more explosions followed. The ship soon lost power. It was obvious that she could not be saved, and destroyers came alongside to take off the survivors. She sank with 216 crewmen who had been killed by the bombs and torpedoes; 2,735 were rescued—plus the captain's pet dog.

But the "Lex" would be avenged. At dawn she and the *Yorktown* had flown off 18 scout planes followed by 82 strike

The burning *Shoho* is bombed and torpedoed by carrier-based planes from the *Yorktown* in the battle of the Coral Sea, May 7, 1942. (National Archives)

Eighteen Type 97 Mk 12 torpedo-bombers (Kates) prepare to launch from the *Zuikaku* in spring 1942. (Kiyokuma Okajima)

aircraft. After a flight of an hour and a quarter they sighted the two Japanese carriers. The *Zuikaku* entered a rain squall and would escape damage. The American fliers fell on the *Shokaku* but scored only three bomb hits which caused minor damage.

The *Shokaku* suffered 109 dead and others injured. Some thirty Japanese planes had been lost in combat during the day, and another heavily damaged 12 were abandoned into the sea after landing. Others that were damaged and had landed on the *Zuikaku* were pushed over the side when she had to recover the *Shokaku*'s planes. With only 39 planes remaining ready for combat, the Japanese decided to withdraw the two carriers from the battle and delay the invasion of Port Moresby. (The day had cost the U.S. Navy 33 planes in combat and another 36 when the *Lexington* went down.)

The *Yorktown* force also withdrew. Sthe was damaged and would need many days in a shipyard before she would be ready for combat. The Coral Sea battle was history's *first* in which the participating ships never saw their opponents; it was fought entirely by their aircraft. And, that first battle was a victory for the Japanese Navy. The small *Shoho* had been sunk while the U.S. Navy lost the large *Lexington*—sometimes called the "Queen of the Flattops"—as well as a destroyer and an oiler. One U.S. carrier was damaged as was one Japanese carrier.

Coral Sea, however, was a strategic victory for the United States. The assault on Port Moresby was turned back, the first major failure in the Japanese plans for conquest. At the same time, the damage to the *Shokaku* and the loss of over 70 first-line carrier planes and many of their pilots meant that neither ship would participate in the forthcoming Battle of Midway, and their absence would have severe consequences for Japan.

The wrecked carrier *Lexington* is covered with smoke and listing heavily on May 8, 1942. (National Archives)

Aichi Type 99 Mk 11 Carrier-based Dive-bomber (D3A1) Cutaway

1 Elevator
2 Elevator trim tab
3 Horizontal stabilizer
4 Rear navigation light
5 Rudder trim tab
6 Rudder
7 Vertical stabilizer
8 Elevator control linkage
9 Rudder control linkage
10 Non-retractable tailwheel
11 Arresting hook control cable
12 Arresting hook (lowered)
13 Arresting hook housing
14 Elevator control rod
15 Rudder control rod
16 Vertical stabilizer root fillet
17 Life raft container
18 Type 90 flare bombs stowage
19 Spare 7.7 mm ammunition magazines
   (97 rounds each)
20 7.7 mm Type 92 (Lewis)
   flexible mounted machine gun
21 Oxygen bottles
22 Machine gun support arms
23 DF receiver
24 Type 94 flame-floats stowage
25 Arresting hook retract lever

26 Navigator's seat
27 Key
28 Navigator's bag
29 Type 97 Model 1 drift sight
30 Wave detector
31 Type 96 *Kuh* (Air) Model 2 wireless set
32 Compass
33 Aerial mast
34 Aerial
35 Roll-over crash pylon
36 Pilot's seat
37 Carbonic acid gas bottles
   (for fire extinguisher and air-bladder)
38 Dynamotor
39 Fuel tank selector
40 Seat height adjustment mechanism
41 Seat belt
42 Hydraulic hand pump
43 Flap control lever
44 Instrument panel
45 Rudder control linkage
46 Link-belt segment discard chute
47 7.7 mm Type 97 (Vickers) machine guns
48 Switchbox
49 Type 95 telescopic bombing/firing sight
50 Sight cap
51 7.7 mm ammunition feed chute
52 Engine bearers
53 Firewall
54 Oil tank
   (74 ltr/19.55 U.S. gal/16.3 Imp gal)
55 Engine accessories

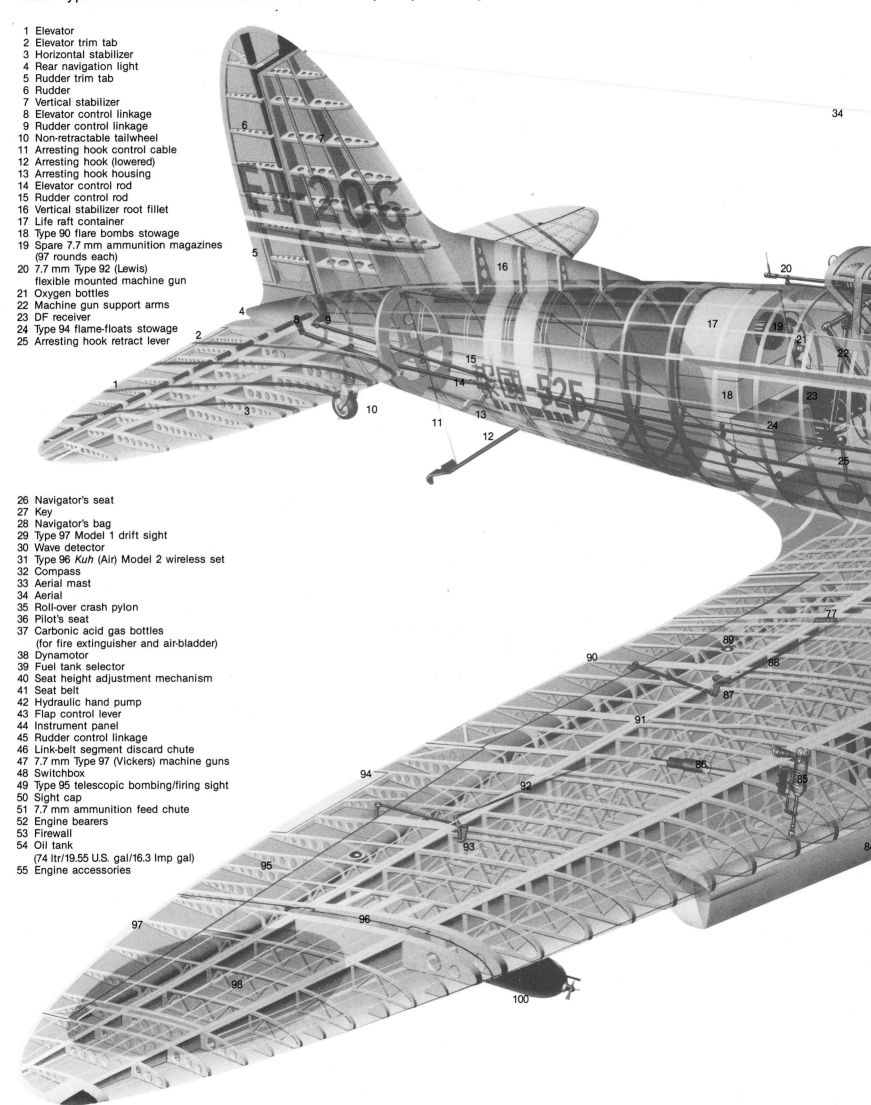

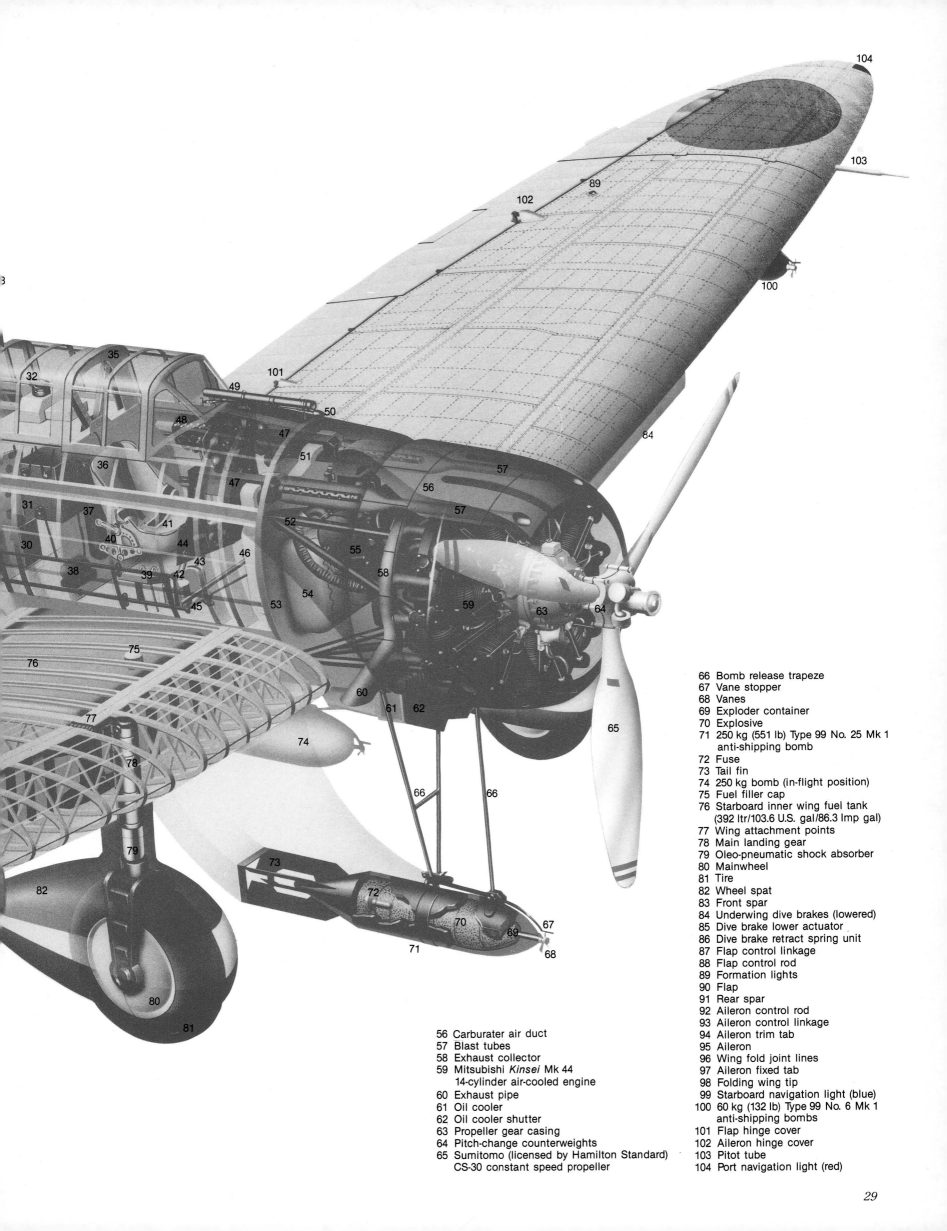

66 Bomb release trapeze
67 Vane stopper
68 Vanes
69 Exploder container
70 Explosive
71 250 kg (551 lb) Type 99 No. 25 Mk 1
   anti-shipping bomb
72 Fuse
73 Tail fin
74 250 kg bomb (in-flight position)
75 Fuel filler cap
76 Starboard inner wing fuel tank
   (392 ltr/103.6 U.S. gal/86.3 Imp gal)
77 Wing attachment points
78 Main landing gear
79 Oleo-pneumatic shock absorber
80 Mainwheel
81 Tire
82 Wheel spat
83 Front spar
84 Underwing dive brakes (lowered)
85 Dive brake lower actuator
86 Dive brake retract spring unit
87 Flap control linkage
88 Flap control rod
89 Formation lights
90 Flap
91 Rear spar
92 Aileron control rod
93 Aileron control linkage
94 Aileron trim tab
95 Aileron
96 Wing fold joint lines
97 Aileron fixed tab
98 Folding wing tip
99 Starboard navigation light (blue)
100 60 kg (132 lb) Type 99 No. 6 Mk 1
    anti-shipping bombs
101 Flap hinge cover
102 Aileron hinge cover
103 Pitot tube
104 Port navigation light (red)

56 Carburater air duct
57 Blast tubes
58 Exhaust collector
59 Mitsubishi *Kinsei* Mk 44
   14-cylinder air-cooled engine
60 Exhaust pipe
61 Oil cooler
62 Oil cooler shutter
63 Propeller gear casing
64 Pitch-change counterweights
65 Sumitomo (licensed by Hamilton Standard)
   CS-30 constant speed propeller

The Battle of Midway

The Battle of Midway was planned by the Japanese Navy to extend Japan's defensive perimeter and to force the still-hurting U.S. Pacific Fleet into a decisive battle against a superior Japanese force. Also, the capture of Midway atoll—1,135 miles (2,100 km) northwest of Pearl Harbor—would deprive the U.S. Navy of a forward base for submarine operations.

When the First Air Fleet and other fleet units returned to Japan in April they underwent a period of overhaul and replenishment. The *Shokaku* and *Zuikaku* had lost a number of planes and pilots in combat while all six large carriers had suffered pilots and planes in operational accidents. There were shortages of replacement pilots and aircraft for the carriers. There was some controversy in the Japanese high command about delaying the Midway operations, but the Doolittle raid ended all discussion.

The Japanese plan called for a diversionary assault in the Aleutian islands. This was to cause the Pacific Fleet's available carriers to steam north. Then, the Japanese main forces would descend on Midway, capturing the island for use as a Japanese air and submarine base. A barrier of submarines would be placed between Midway and Hawaii to warn of the approach of U.S. ships. When they did come, the submarines would attack, and then the Japanese carriers and battleships would pound the surviving U.S. ships. Once Midway was captured consideration could be given to an eventual assault on Oahu and its naval base of Pearl Harbor.

The fleets assembling to assault Midway were impressive. Also, new carriers had joined the Japanese fleet, the 24,140-ton *Junyo* and the light carrier *Ryuho* of 13,360 tons. The *Junyo* had been laid down in 1939 as a passenger liner intended for wartime conversion to a carrier. The *Ryuho* was built as a submarine tender, completed in 1934, but rebuilt as a carrier in 1941–1942. These ships normally embarked 48 and 24 planes, respectively.

From the outset the Japanese plan was flawed. The submarines were late in deploying. The ships for the assault on Midway were divided into several forces, being unable to provide mutual support and unable to communicate without breaking radio silence. And, unknown to the Japanese, U.S. Navy code breakers at Peal Harbor knew most of the plan.

By early June the Northern Force was heading toward the Aleutians to begin the battle. The carriers *Junyo* and *Ryujo*, accompanied by cruisers and destroyers, would support that invasion. Three separate forces were converging on Midway:

The *Main Force*, with seven battleships and screening units, had the escort carrier *Hosho* to provide air support.

The *Invasion Force*, with 19 transports and cargo ships carrying 5,000 assault troops, had the light carrier *Zuiho* plus two battleships, ten cruisers, and many destroyers and support ships.

The *Carrier Striking Force* had the large carriers *Akagi*, *Kaga*, *Hiryu*, and *Soryu*, with two battleships, a pair of heavy cruisers, a light cruiser, and 12 destroyers.

Thus the Japanese had five large and three smaller carriers committed to the operation, plus 11 battleships and an armada of lesser warships. To contest the assault on Midway and the Aleutians the United States had the *Enterprise* and *Hor-* *net*, which had been too late for the Coral Sea battle when they returned from the Doolittle raid, and the damaged *Yorktown*. It was estimated that the *Yorktown* required 90 days in a shipyard to ready her for combat. When she entered Pearl Harbor 1,400 workers poured over her and 2½ days later she was ready for sea. If the battle lasted a week or was delayed, the *Saratoga*, coming out from the U.S. West Coast, might reach the battle in time. (But then the *Shokaku* and *Zuikaku* might also be able to reach the battle.) There were no fast battleships available to operate with the carriers; eight cruisers and 17 destroyers would screen the flattops. Several U.S. submarines would serve as a forward barrier, but like most of the Japanese submarines, they would have essentially no role in the coming battle. On Midway was a large number of Navy, Army, and Marine aircraft that would participate in the battle.

The balance of forces was described by American author Herman Wouk in his novel *War and Remembrance*: "The *Hornet*, the *Enterprise*, with possibly the patched leaky *Yorktown* and their meager train, against that Japanese armada! At least eight carriers, perhaps ten battleships, only God could know how many cruisers, destroyers, submarines! As a fleet problem, it was too lopsided for any peacetime empire to propose."

In some respects the most important "weapon" available to the U.S. was intelligence, which permitted the most effective deployment of available ships. The *Enterprise* and *Hornet* with 158 planes sailed from Pearl Harbor on May 28, followed on May 30 by the *Yorktown* with 75 more planes for a total of 233.

As the Japanese ships approached Midway, PBY Catalina flying boats from the island sighted the transports of the invasion force. Immediately long-range Army B-17 bombers from Midway began attacks on the Japanese ships. These and other Army strikes accomplished nothing at Midway except to confuse the issue.

Early on June 4 the Carrier Striking Force, with 225 planes on the decks of the four carriers, began launching a massive strike against Midway, to destroy the airfield and soften up the defenses. One hundred and eight planes began the 210 miles (390 km) flight to Midway. Meanwhile, scout planes from the carriers as well as accompanying cruisers were sent out to seek any U.S. ships that might be approaching the Japanese carriers. Perhaps the most fatal flaw in the Japanese plan occurred when the cruiser planes were delayed and then one turned back with engine trouble. No replacement plane was launched. (Meanwhile, Midway-based PBYs were scouting for the Japanese, and at 5:52 a.m. one of these sighted the Japanese carriers.)

At 6:30 a.m. on June 4 the Japanese planes began bombing Midway. Navy and Marine fighters attempted to intercept them, and there was lively anti-aircraft fire from the island. Four Japanese planes were shot down as were 15 of the U.S. fighters. As the planes flew back to the carriers the fatal message was sent that another raid was needed against the island.

This message and the periodic (and ineffective) attacks by Navy, Marine, and Army planes from Midway that were now being made against the carriers convinced the Carrier Striking Force commander that another raid was needed against the island. Another 103 planes were on his deck, armed with bombs and torpedoes to strike out against any U.S. ships found in the area. After some deliberation, he ordered the 43 Kates to have their torpedoes removed and bombs fitted for attacking Midway.

While this was going on the Japanese carriers began to receive reports from their scout planes: American warships were some 200 miles (370 km) east of the carriers. At first there was no report of carriers, but then one flattop was sighted. Now there were the first signs of panic. The torpedoes that had been removed were ordered put back on the Kates. And the fighters that had been intended for the second strike were being sent up to combat the continuous attacks by Midway-based planes. In the midst of this tumult, the returning first Midway strike force had to be recovered.

At 10:20 a.m. the Japanese carriers were ready to launch additional defensive fighters over the fleet. As the first plane was leaving the flagship *Akagi*'s deck, a few seconds later a bomb slammed into the ship. The plane that had released it was an SBD from the U.S. carrier *Enterprise*.

Earlier that morning, based on the PBY sighting reports and then those of the other Midway-based planes, the U.S. carriers had begun launching strikes against the Japanese carriers. First the *Enterprise* and *Hornet* flew off a total of 117 aircraft. Two hours later the *Yorktown* began flying off another 35 palnes. The enemy carriers were reported to be 200 miles (370 km) away, slightly beyond the round-trip range of the TBD torpedo planes. But they might be able to land at Midway after the battle.

The differing speeds of the U.S. aircraft types and the lack of coordination led to the various squadrons from the three carriers becoming widely separated. The first planes to arrive at the expected position of the Japanese carriers found the sea empty; the PBY's report had been in error. Thirteen SBDs from the *Hornet* flew to Midway; the 10 F4F fighters and two other SBDs exhausted their fuel and came down at sea. Another 20 SBDs from the *Hornet* and *Enterprise* returned to their carriers.

The *Soryu* makes a complete circle trying to avoid bombs from Midway-based B-17E heavy bombers on June 4, 1942. (National Archives)

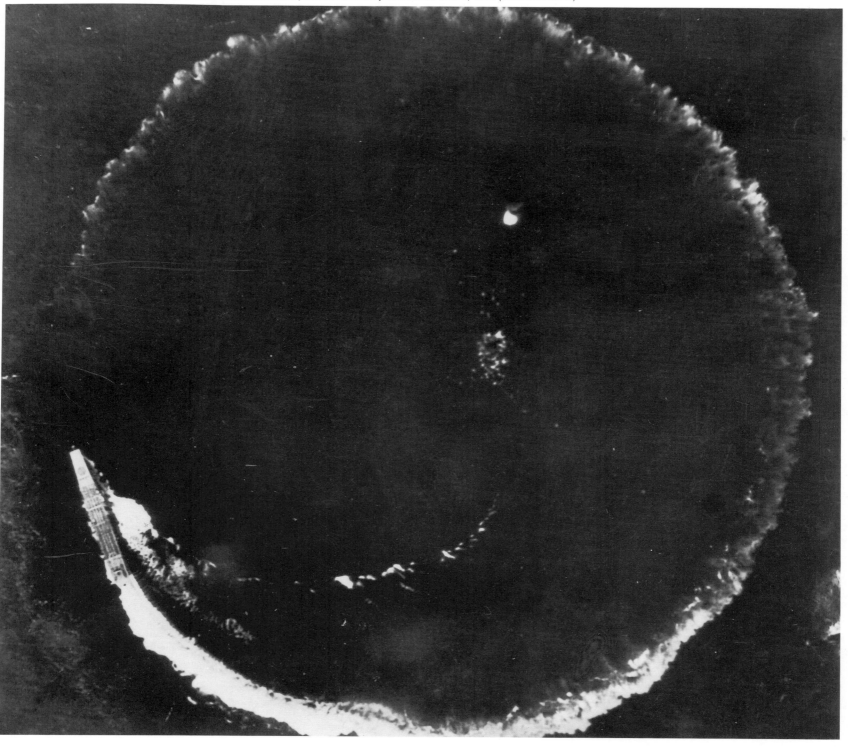

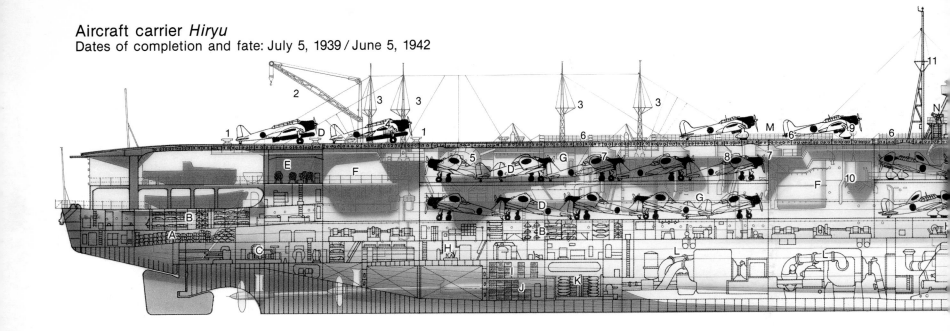

Aircraft carrier *Hiryu*
Dates of completion and fate: July 5, 1939 / June 5, 1942

The U.S. torpedo planes—41 TBD Devastators—were the first U.S. carrier planes to find the Japanese carriers. The three squadrons, one from each carrier, attacked. Flying low and slow as they lined up for releasing their torpedoes, these planes were shot out of the sky. All 15 TBDs from the *Hornet* were shot down as were all 12 from the *Yorktown* and 10 from the "Big E." Only four planes survived from the 41! None of their torpedoes hit the widely maneuvering carriers. Their efforts, however, forced the defending Zeros down to wave-top level and exhausted much of their fuel.

When the 33 SBD dive bombers from the *Enterprise* found the Japanese carriers they met essentially no opposition. At 10:26 a.m. their first bomb hit the *Akagi*. Within moments she was devastated by three bombs; the nearby *Kaga* was hit by four direct hits. Moments later the carrier *Hornet*'s 17 SBDs attacked the *Soryu*, scoring three hits. The Japanese carriers were especially vulnerable because of the fueled and armed planes in their hangars. All three ships were soon blazing infernos. Only the *Hiryu* escaped—for a short time.

Sixty-seven U.S. carrier planes were lost to enemy action and by coming down at sea when their fuel ran out. Immediate preparations were made for another strike against the one or two possible surviving Japanese flattops. In response to

the earlier sighting of U.S. carriers, at 10:58 a.m. the *Hiryu* flew off a small strike of six Zeros and 18 Val dive bombers. These planes found the *Yorktown*, and six were able to attack, scoring three hits that inflicted severe damage on the ship. Meanwhile, the admiral in the *Hiryu* learned belatedly that there were two more U.S. carriers in the area. He had only six fighters and ten torpedo planes ready to launch.

After recovering their planes, the *Enterprise-Hornet* group made additional launches, and at 5 p.m., 24 SBDs from the "Big E" found the *Hiryu*. In a few minutes she too was shattered by four direct hits. Soon afterwards the *Hornet* dive bombers arrived on the scene, but there were no more Japanese carriers of the First Air Fleet to attack.

Salvage efforts were under way on the damaged *Yorktown*, and it looked as if the carrier could be saved. Early on the morning of June 5 the *Yorktown* was lying dead in the water with a destroyer alongside to provide electrical power while a tug was taking the flattop in tow. Five other destroyers circled them on anti-submarine patrol. Astutely commanded, the Japanese submarine I-168 approached and fired a salvo of four torpedoes. Moments later the destroyer sank; the *Yorktown* survived the night, her listing increasing, until she sank on the morning of June 7. The I-168 escaped the cascade of depth

Type 97 Mk 12 torpedo-bomber (Kate) from the *Hiryu* approaches the *Yorktown* through heavy anti-aircraft fire on June 4. (National Archives)

The damaged carrier *Yorktown* is surrounded by shell-bursts against the *Hiryu*'s aircraft. (National Archives)

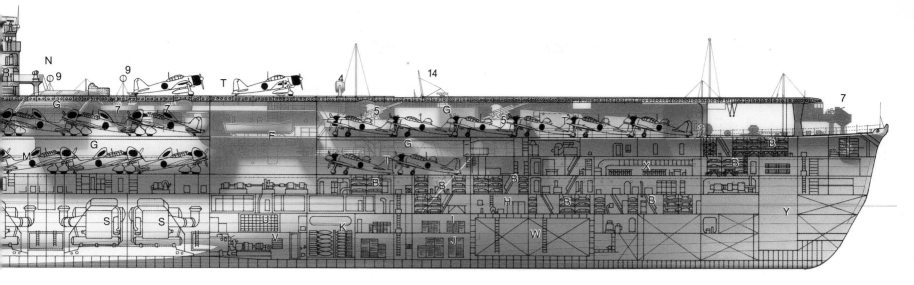

Displacement
Standard: 17,300 tons
Trial: 20,250 tons
Dimensions
Length on design waterline: 222.0 m (728.4 ft)
Length overall: 227.35 m (745.9 ft)
Beam: 22.32 m (73.2 ft)
Draught: 7.84 m (25.7 ft)
Flight deck: 216.9 m (711.6 ft) × 27.0 m (88.6 ft)
Machinery
4-shaft geared turbines, 8 boilers: 15,300 shp,
34.3 knots (63.5 km/h)
Armament
: 12 × 5 in (12.7 cm) L/40 anti-aircraft guns
 31 × 25 mm anti-aircraft cannon
Aircraft (on Dec. 7, 1941)
Attacker: 18 plus 3 (reserved)
Dive-bomber: 18 plus 3 (reserved)
Fighter: 18 plus 3 (reserved)
Complement
: 1,101

1 Landing lights
2 Boat and aircraft crane
3 Long range wireless rigs
4 Type 92 110 cm (43.3 in) searchlights
5 Twin 12.7 cm (5.0 in) Type 89 anti-aircraft gun mounts
6 Safety nets
7 Triple 25 mm Type 96 anti-aircraft machine gun mounts
8 Type 95 fire control director for 25 mm machine guns
9 Direction finder antennas
10 Direction finder control room
11 Signal flag mast
12 Aircraft control station
13 Type 94 fire control directors for 12.7 cm guns
14 Hinged blast deflector

A Relish storerooms
B Crew's space
C Steering gear
D Type 97 Mk 12 (Model 3)
   carrier-based torpedo-bombers (B5N2/Kate)

E Aircraft engine workshop
F Aircraft elevators
G Hangars
H Arresting wire control rooms
I 12.7 cm (5 in) magazines
J 25 mm magazines
K Bomb rooms
L Engine rooms
M Type 99 Mk 11 carrier-based dive-bombers (D3A1/Val)
N Type 94 searchlight control directors
O Weather station
P Conning tower
Q Control room
R Operations room/Chart house
S Boiler room
T Type 0 Mk 21 carrier-based fighters (A6M2/Zero)
U Powder magazine
V Generator room
W Oil fuel stowages
X Officers' room
Y Anchor chain storehouse

charges sent against her; her captain had scored the only successes of the entire Japanese fleet.

In the Aleutians the Japanese force, with the carriers *Junyo* and *Ryujo* providing 76 aircraft, was able to strike the U.S. base at Dutch Harbor. Then, reinforced by the light carrier *Zuiho* and other ships from the Midway invasion force, on June 7 Japanese captured the Aleutian islands of Kiska and Attu, which were undefended. The Japanese held this toehold on the American continent until mid-1943.

The Battle of Midway was the second carrier-versus-carrier battle of the war. It was the first decisive defeat suffered by the Japanese navy since 1592 when the Korean admiral Yi-sun defeated a Japanese invasion force under Hideyoshi off the Korean coast. The battle cost the Japanese four large carriers and a heavy cruiser sunk, and several ships were damaged. All 250 aircraft on the Japanese carriers were lost (the carriers had

The doomed *Hiryu* on June 5. This Photograph was taken by a Type 96 torpedo-bomber of the *Hosho* from 100 m (330 ft) above the water. (Yoji Watanabe)

The Battle of Midway (June 4, 1942)

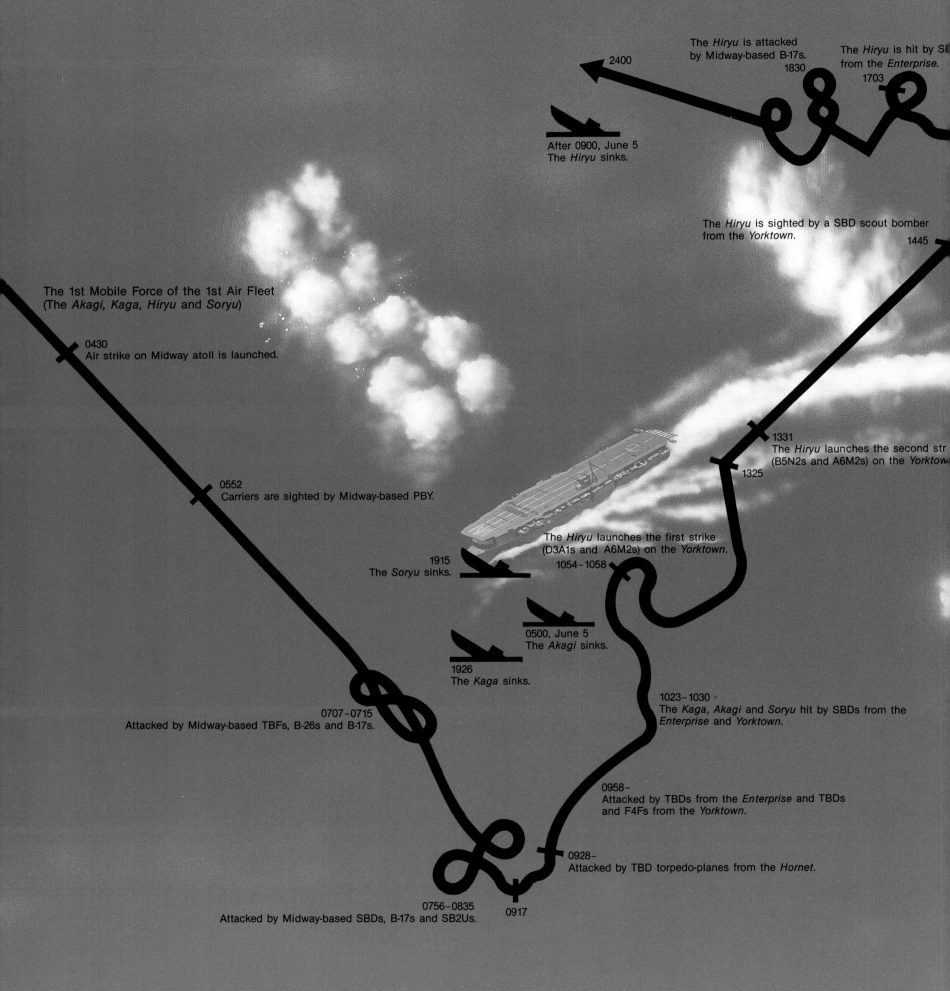

The *Hiryu* is attacked by Midway-based B-17s.
1830

The *Hiryu* is hit by SE from the *Enterprise*.
1703

2400

After 0900, June 5
The *Hiryu* sinks.

The *Hiryu* is sighted by a SBD scout bomber from the *Yorktown*.
1445

The 1st Mobile Force of the 1st Air Fleet
(The *Akagi, Kaga, Hiryu* and *Soryu*)

0430
Air strike on Midway atoll is launched.

1331
The *Hiryu* launches the second str (B5N2s and A6M2s) on the *Yorktow*

1325

0552
Carriers are sighted by Midway-based PBY.

The *Hiryu* launches the first strike (D3A1s and A6M2s) on the *Yorktown*.
1054–1058

1915
The *Soryu* sinks.

0500, June 5
The *Akagi* sinks.

1926
The *Kaga* sinks.

1023–1030
The *Kaga, Akagi* and *Soryu* hit by SBDs from the *Enterprise* and *Yorktown*.

0707–0715
Attacked by Midway-based TBFs, B-26s and B-17s.

0958–
Attacked by TBDs from the *Enterprise* and TBDs and F4Fs from the *Yorktown*.

0928–
Attacked by TBD torpedo-planes from the *Hornet*.

0756–0835
Attacked by Midway-based SBDs, B-17s and SB2Us.

0917

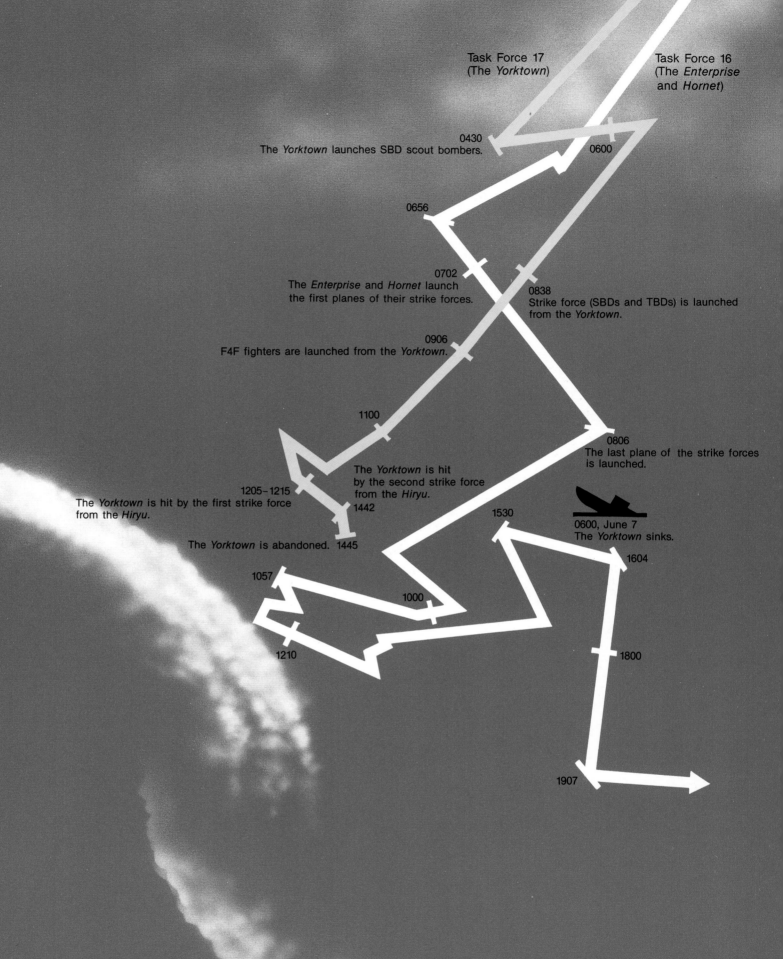

Task Force 17
(The *Yorktown*)

Task Force 16
(The *Enterprise*
and *Hornet*)

0430
The *Yorktown* launches SBD scout bombers.

0600

0656

0702
The *Enterprise* and *Hornet* launch
the first planes of their strike forces.

0838
Strike force (SBDs and TBDs) is launched
from the *Yorktown*.

0906
F4F fighters are launched from the *Yorktown*.

1100

1550

0806
The last plane of the strike forces
is launched.

The *Yorktown* is hit
by the second strike force
from the *Hiryu*.

1205–1215
The *Yorktown* is hit by the first strike force
from the *Hiryu*.

1442

1530

0600, June 7
The *Yorktown* sinks.

The *Yorktown* is abandoned. 1445

1604

1057

1000

1210

1800

1907

Bomb laden SBD-3s flying over their targets—the heavy cruisers *Mogami* and *Mikuma*—on June 6, 1942. The picture was enlarged from a 16 mm movie film. (National Archives)

25 fighters to be sent ashore after Midway was captured). More than 2,000 men died in the carriers, among them highly skilled pilots, air crewmen, and mechanics, plus about a thousand men in the cruiser that was sunk by carrier planes on June 6.

The U.S. Navy lost one carrier and one destroyer; only a few men died with the *Yorktown* while the destroyer lost 81 men (plus a few who later succumbed to wounds.) The U.S. carriers lost 109 planes—the losses of Midway-based planes pushed the total to about 150—with many of their pilots being rescued. It was an overwhelming victory for the U.S. Navy.

Midway has been called the "turning point of the war." It was; never again would the Japanese Navy have the offensive. But it was not the battle that changed the course of the war. The course was decided long before; the manpower and industrial base of the United States would permit no other outcome if the Americans persisted. The battle found the Japanese Empire at the height of its strength and the United States at near its nadir. Japan could only grow weaker and the United States only stronger as the war progressed. And aircraft carriers would be an important measure of the two nations' military strength.

The damaged heavy cruiser *Mikuma* after attack of SBD dive bombers. (National Archives)

The Tide Turns

After the Battle of Midway the United States had gained the initiative in the Pacific. The Japanese carrier force had been badly hurt while, despite the loss of the *Lexington* and *Yorktown*, the U.S. Navy had four large carriers in the Pacific after the battle: The *Enterprise*, *Hornet*, and *Saratoga* plus the *Wasp*, recently arrived from the Atlantic. With the *Wasp* came the new, fast (27-knot) battleship *North Carolina*. She and other ships of this type would often operate closely with the fast carriers, their massive batteries of 5 in (12.7 cm), 40 mm, and 20 mm guns adding considerably to the defenses of carrier task forces.

The Anglo-American high command had decided that Germany was the No.1 enemy and that the principal emphasis in the war would be in the Atlantic-Mediterranean, with the allies to go on the offensive before the end of 1942 with an invasion of North Afirca. But in the Pacific a limited offensive could be undertaken. The fast carriers would be the key to such an offensive because of the large size of the remaining Japanese fleet and the large number of land bases across the Pacific available to the Japanese.

The first objective in the American offensive would be the island of Guadalcanal and the smaller, adjacent Tulagi, in the Solomon Islands, northeast of the Coral Sea. The Japanese had established a seaplane base at Tulagi and were building an airfield on Guadalcanal that could be used to support another attempt against the Allied base at Port Moresby.

By early August a U.S. Marine assault force was steaming into the Solomon area, screened by three U.S. carriers, the *Enterprise*, *Saratoga*, and *Wasp*. Although the airfield on Guadalcanal was not ready for planes, Guadalcanal was within range of Japanese planes based at Rabaul on New Britain. The landings began at 6:13 a.m. on August 7, catching the defenders by surprise.

An immediate strike of twin-engine bombers and Zeros was launched from Rabaul. The U.S. carrier planes easily fought off the attackers as they did a second raid from Rabaul. Fearful of continued raids, the U.S. carrier force commander withdrew southward. In their absence, on the night of August 8–9, a Japanese cruiser–destroyer force entered the area and quickly sank four U.S. and Australian cruisers and damaged other ships without loss.

This set the pattern for seven months of sea battles for Guadalcanal. Japanese land-based aircraft and surface warships, the latter steaming into the area at night, attempted to turn the tide in favor of the Japanese, often in support of troops being shipped into the island. Periodically the Japanese sent aircraft carriers into the battle, and in late August the veteran fleet carriers *Shokaku* and *Zuikaku* and the light carrier *Ryujo* were sent to support reinforcement of their troops on Guadalcanal. On their decks were 177 aircraft (with more available at Rabaul).

Forewarned, the U.S. Navy had its three carriers in the area ready for battle in the Eastern Solomons. They had 256 aircraft on board. On the morning of August 23 the *Saratoga* began history's third carrier-versus-carrier battle when she launched 37 bombers toward reported Japanese transports followed by 23 Marine planes from Guadalcanal (Henderson Field). Hampered by bad weather, these planes missed the transports and all returned to Henderson Field.

Realizing that the Americans now knew of the forces headed toward Guadalcanal, the Japanese sent the carrier *Ryujo* into the area as "bait" for the U.S. carriers while the larger *Shokaku* and *Zuikaku* stood ready to pounce once the U.S. flattops were located.

Without detailed knowledge of the Japanese forces, the U.S. commander had the *Hornet* group refuel to the south, leaving only two carriers and their escorts steaming east of Guadalcanal. On the morning of the 24th U.S. PBY Catalina flying boats sighted the carrier *Ryujo* some 280 miles (520 km) from the U.S. carriers. The *Enterprise* and *Saratoga* both flew off large search-attack flights of SBD Dauntlesses and the new TBF Avenger torpedo planes. A total of 61 bomb-laden U.S. planes were aloft seeking the *Ryujo*.

Meanwhile, the *Ryujo* had sent off 21 planes to strike Henderson Field. Early in the afternoon she was found by U.S. carrier planes, as were the two larger Japanese carriers some distance behind her. The SBD pilots pushed over into dives while

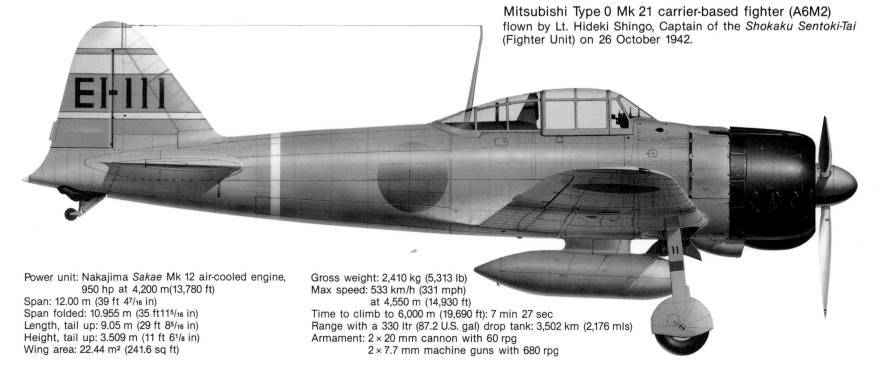

Mitsubishi Type 0 Mk 21 carrier-based fighter (A6M2) flown by Lt. Hideki Shingo, Captain of the *Shokaku Sentoki-Tai* (Fighter Unit) on 26 October 1942.

Power unit: Nakajima *Sakae* Mk 12 air-cooled engine, 950 hp at 4,200 m(13,780 ft)
Span: 12.00 m (39 ft 4⁷/₁₆ in)
Span folded: 10.955 m (35 ft11⁵/₁₆ in)
Length, tail up: 9.05 m (29 ft 8⁵/₁₆ in)
Height, tail up: 3.509 m (11 ft 6¹/₈ in)
Wing area: 22.44 m² (241.6 sq ft)

Gross weight: 2,410 kg (5,313 lb)
Max speed: 533 km/h (331 mph) at 4,550 m (14,930 ft)
Time to climb to 6,000 m (19,690 ft): 7 min 27 sec
Range with a 330 ltr (87.2 U.S. gal) drop tank: 3,502 km (2,176 mls)
Armament: 2 × 20 mm cannon with 60 rpg
2 × 7.7 mm machine guns with 680 rpg

Grumman F4F-4 Wildcat
of VF-10 aboard the Enterprise on 26 October 1942.

Power unit: Pratt & Whitney R-1830-86 Twin Wasp air-cooled
engine, 1,200 hp at 1,800 ft (550 m)
Span: 38 ft 0 in (11.58 m)
Span folded: 14 ft 4 in (4.37 m)
Length, tail up: 29 ft 0 in (8.84 m)
Height, tail down, propeller vertical : 11 ft 4 in (3.45 m)

Wing area: 260 sq ft (24.15 m²)
Gross weight: 7,975 lb (3,617 kg)
Max speed: 320 mph (515 km/h) at 18,800 ft (5,730 m)
Time to climb to 20,000 ft (6,100 m): 12 min 24 sec
Range with two 58 U.S. gal (220 ltr) drop tank: 1,275 mls
(2,052 km)
Armament: 6 × 12.7 mm machine guns with 240 rpg

the TBFs streaked low over the water amid Zeros and anti-aircraft fire from the carriers and their escorting ships. The *Ryujo* was smothered by several near misses and one torpedo hit. The Americans were unable to hit the larger ships.

No U.S. planes were lost in these attacks, but the *Ryujo* had served her purpose as bait. Japanese scouts found the U.S. carriers, and beginning about 3 p.m. the two larger carriers launched 37 aircraft. Just before 5 p.m. the Vals and Kates attacked. Fifty-three Wildcats were defending the U.S. ships.

At 5 : 14 the *Enterprise* took her first bomb hit, followed less than a minute later by another bomb striking ten feet (3 m) from where the first had struck. A few minutes later she took a third hit. The "Big E" was the only U.S. ship hit. She was badly hurt, listing, and in flames. Then her rudder jammed. At this point a second, 36-plane strike from the undamaged *Shokaku* and *Zuikaku* was approaching. But fortune smiled on the Americans, and the Japanese planes missed the U.S. ships by about 50 miles (90 km).

Aircraft from the *Saratoga* sought out the enemy carriers but found only a seaplane carrier and other ships, which escaped damage. Finally, the two U.S. carriers withdrew to the south. The Battle of the Eastern Solomons was over. The *Enterprise* was heavily damaged, and 17 carrier planes were missing; the Japanese had lost the *Ryujo* and 59 carrier planes, plus a few seaplanes and Rabaul-based bombers. The Japanese losses were greater, and their transports were forced to unload their troops into destroyers for high-speed runs into Guadalcanal, without their heavy equipment. The Americans held Henderson Field and continued to press against the Japanese troops.

The *Enterprise* withdrew to Pearl Harbor for repairs. The *Hornet* arrived in the area, rebuilding U.S. carrier strength to three ships. They were kept well south of Rabaul-based aircraft. On August 31 the Japanese submarine I-26 made a torpedo attack on the *Saratoga* and scored a hit on the U.S. navy's largest warship. This, the second torpedo hit she had taken in

the war, inflicted minor damage, but her sensitive turbo-electric propulsion system required three months in a shipyard to set right. Most of her planes were sent to Henderson Field, where they joined Marine fighters and bombers as well as planes flown ashore from the "Big E."

A few days later another submarine fired at the *Hornet*, but a fast-thinking SBD pilot who had just taken off dropped his depth bomb and made the torpedo run wide of its target. On the afternoon of September 15 the *Wasp* and *Hornet* were steaming toward Guadalcanal to cover U.S. transports. The carriers and their escorts were in two groups. On September 15 the Japanese I-19 fired what was probably the most effective torpedo salvo in submarine history. As the submarine's captain made a submerged approach on the *Wasp* group, he was unaware that another U.S. task group with the carrier *Hornet* and the battleship *North Carolina* was beyond periscope view. In all 23 American warships were within range of his torpedoes.

Six torpedoes were fired by the I-19 at 2 : 42 p.m. Three slammed into the side of the carrier *Wasp*. Three others missed that ship and raced across toward the other task group, more than five miles (9 km) away. One of these passed under the *North Carolina*, one struck the battleship, and one struck a destroyer. The *Wasp* was wracked by explosions and sank five hours later. The damaged *North Carolina* and the destroyer limped away, the smaller ship sinking from her wounds before she could reach a shipyard. The submarine I-15 made a torpedo attack on the *Hornet* at about this time, but her torpedoes all missed. The *Wasp* sank with the loss of 193 of her crew of more than 2,200 men. With her loss, the *Hornet* was the only fully operational U.S. carrier in the Pacific.

The Japanese high command was planning another major foray into the Solomons. This time the four carriers would be available—the veteran *Shokaku* and *Zuikaku*, the smaller *Junyo*, and the light *Zuiho*. They embarked 216 aircraft. Their firepower was backed up by four battleships and eight heavy cruisers.

To counter this thrust the U.S. Navy could assemble the carriers *Hornet* and hastily repaired *Enterprise* supported by one battleship, four heavy cruisers, and several anti-aircraft cruisers and destroyers. There were 171 planes in the U.S. carriers as they approached the Santa Cruz islands. On October 24–25 the two opposing fleets searched for each other, and a few attacks, mostly by land-based aircraft, failed to inflict any damage. Early on the 26th the *Enterprise* flew off 16 SBDs, each with a 500 lb (227 kg) bomb, to search for the Japanese. Several found the *Zuiho* and scored one hit.

Also that morning, after a Japanese floatplane found the U.S. carrier *Hornet*, the Japanese carriers flew off a 62-plane strike (some from the *Zuiho* before she was hit). While they were en route the U.S. ships launched a 73-plane raid against the Japanese. The two groups of planes passed as they flew to their targets. There were some engagements, and both sides lost a couple of planes. A second strike, with 44 planes, was also sent off by the Japanese ships.

The Japanese struck first in the Battle of Santa Cruz. The *Enterprise* was in a squall, and the full force of the attack fell on the *Hornet*. She took six bomb and two torpedo hits, plus several near misses, and two damaged planes crashed on her deck. The *Hornet* was ablaze from stem to stern, dead in the water, and listing. (The cost to the Japanese squadrons/flying units was 25 planes lost in combat and another 13 that came down at sea when returning to their ships.)

Meanwhile, the U.S. strike found its target. The *Shokaku* was hit with four 1,000 lb (454 kg) bombs, and several other ships were damaged. The *Shokaku* withdrew from the battle. The *Zuikaku* and *Junyo* were unscathed and still in the fight.

The second Japanese strike of 44 planes found the blazing *Hornet* as well as the undamaged "Big E." Three bombs hit the *Enterprise*, but she was able to evade others as well as nine torpedoes launched against her. The raid cost the Japanese 24 planes, but the *Enterprise* was damaged. (A third Japanese raid of 29 planes from the *Junyo* inflicted no further damage.) A cruiser took the *Hornet* in tow, and the damaged *Enterprise* limped along behind her.

The Japanese still had the *Junyo* and *Zuikaku* operational, and although a total of 78 aircraft were lost in the morning strikes, they flew off a 15-plane strike early in the afternoon. These fell on the *Hornet*, hitting her with a bomb and a torpedo. The carrier was ordered abandoned. This was followed by a 10-plane strike that landed another bomb on the *Hornet*. The carrier was dying, and U.S. ships sent her to the bottom. She was the fourth U.S. carrier to be lost in the war; the Japanese had also lost four large carriers (at Midway) plus two light carriers.

The Battle of Santa Cruz had cost the U.S. Navy a carrier sunk and another damaged, with the loss of 74 planes, plus a destroyer sunk. The Japanese suffered two carriers heavily damaged plus 90 planes lost. The Japanese command shifted to nighttime raids and reinforcement efforts for Guadalcanal after the Santa Cruz battle. Carriers provided distant cover. On the U.S. side the lone *Enterprise* was kept south of the Guadalcanal area, staging her planes through Henderson Field to strike at the Japanese.

The conflict for Guadalcanal continued until February 1943, when the Japanese evacuated what troops it could from the battle-torn island. The campaign had cost the United States two carriers, the Japanese one, plus several damaged on both sides. While the critical carrier battles of 1942 were being fought in the Pacific, American shipyards were building more major warships—including aircraft carriers—than all of the rest of the world's navies combined. In fall and summer of 1940, in

Type 97 Mk 12 torpedo-bombers (Kates) and Type 99 Mk 11 dive-bombers (Vals) attack simultaneously on the *Hornet* during the Battle of Santa Cruz. (National Archives)

SBD dive-bombers onboard the newly commissioned *Lexington* (CV-16), one of the *Essex*-class fast carriers, in the Atlantic on May 11, 1943. (National Archives)

response to the fall of France, the Americans had ordered no less than 11 fast carriers. (Another 11 were ordered in the first year of the war, but only four were finished before the war ended.) These ships were all of the *Essex* class, 27,100-ton, 872 ft (266 m) or 888 ft (271 m) fast carriers that could easily accommodate 90 aircraft.

Also, in 1941 the Navy reordered nine 10,000-ton light cruisers, some not yet started, to be completed as fast light carriers. Displacing 11,000 tons in the CVL configuration, these 610 ft (186 m) ships could carry 35 planes each.

By mid-June 1943 the U.S. Navy was able to undertake a new offensive in the Central Pacific with four fast carriers and five light carriers available; some had been renamed while being built to honor carriers lost in the first year of war:

CV-9   *Essex*
CV-10   *Yorktown*
CV-16   *Lexington*
CV-17   *Bunker Hill*
CVL-22 *Independence*
CVL-23 *Princeton*
CVL-24 *Belleau Wood*
CVL-25 *Cowpens*
CVL-26 *Monterey*

Simultaneous with these carriers, a new Navy fighter became available, the F6F Hellcat, the first U.S. Fighter capable of defeating a Zero under almost any conditions. A leading Japanese pilot declared, "Of the many American fighter planes we encountered in the Pacific, the Hellcat was the only aircraft

which could acquit itself with distinction in a fighter-*vs*-fighter dogfight." The other planes on their decks were the now-familiar SBD Dauntless dive bombers and TBF/TBM Avenger torpedo planes (the two designations indicating different manufacturers of the same disign.)

In September 1943 these ships began flying strikes against isolated Japanese atolls, primarily to give the ship and air crews combat experience with light opposition. More ambitious raids followed, including one against Rabaul while U.S. troops moved farther up the Solomon island chain. In reaction to these raids, the Japanese sent the newly rebuilt aircraft squadrons (flying units) of the *Shokaku* and *Zuikaku* to Rabaul, and they suffered significant losses.

On November 19 the U.S. Navy began the Central Pacific campaign with attacks against Japanese air bases in the Gilbert and Marshall island groups. The U.S. task forces, with the older *Enterprise* and *Saratoga*, had six large and five light carriers with almost 700 aircraft—the largest concentration of carrier air power ever assembled by any navy. These planes swept away all semblance of air opposition, and U.S. Marines stormed ashore on Tarawa and Makin. The few Japanese planes that were able to reach the U.S. task forces succeeded only in torpedoing the CVL *Independence*. She lost 17 men dead and more injured but was able to steam out of the area for repairs.

With the assault force were eight small escort carriers. These so-called "jeep" carriers had about 30 fighters and bombers, except for two that carried fighters to be flown ashore when airfields became available. These planes provided close air sup-

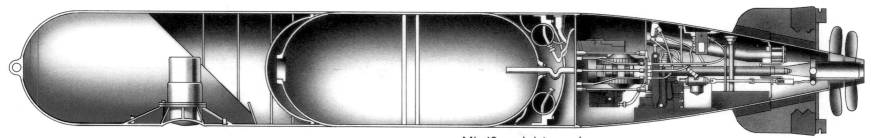

port and air patrols for the amphibious ships, freeing the larger flattops for other operations. The only major Japanese success against these CVEs came when a Japanese submarine torpedoed and sank the *Liscome Bay* (CVE-56).

The Japanese high command could only respond to the assault with submarines as there were no major air or surface forces capable of engaing the U.S. fleet. The U.S. drive in the Central Pacific continued. Kwajalein was assaulted by U.S. Marines on January 31, 1944.

More carriers were joining the U.S. fleet: the *Essex*-class ships *Intrepid* (CV-11), *Hornet* (CV-12), and *Wasp* (CV-18), and the light carriers *Langley* (CVL-27), *Cabot* (CVL-28), *Bataan* (CVL-29), and *San Jacinto* (CVL-30).

The major Japanese fleet base of Truk in the Caroline Islands was attacked by nine U.S. carriers on February 17–18. The surprise attack began with an early fighter sweep across the airfields. During two days the carrier planes destroyed a light cruiser and three destroyers in the harbor, a training cruiser and another destroyer at sea, and sank 31 merchant ships; about 250 aircraft were destroyed in the air and on the ground. The only damage to the U.S. carriers was slight damage to the *Intrepid* from an aerial torpedo. Twenty-five American planes were lost, with many of their pilots rescued. Truk was no longer useable as a Japanese fleet base.

Six of the U.S. carriers then turned north, and at dawn of February 22 their planes struck Saipan in the Marianas, only 1,460 miles (2,350 km) from the capital city of Tokyo. On the runways were not only the Saipan garrison's planes but many carrier planes that had been training in Japan but flown down to the Marianas after the raid on Truk, the first arriving two days earlier! About 145 Japanese planes were destroyed on the ground and in the air at the cost of six U.S. carrier planes. Eleven ships were also sunk by U.S. air attack.

Mk 13 aerial torpedo
Length overall: 13 ft 5 in (4.09 m)
Diameter: 22.4 in (56.9 cm)
Total weight: 2,216 lb (1,005 kg)
Explosive charge: 600 lb (272 kg) Torpex
Range: 6,300 yds (5,760 m) at 33.5 kts (62 km/h)

A Grumman TBF-1 Avenger dropping an Mk 13 aerial torpedo. (National Archives)

By the spring 1944 U.S. Marines had captured the key Japanese atolls in the Marshall archipelago as well as Eniwetok, several hundred miles farther west. These operations cost the Japanese Navy considerable numbers of carrier planes and pilots. Although the high command sought to stop the American advances with a surface fleet, a combination of aircraft losses and lack of adequate intelligence on U.S. plans prevented any response except with submarine attacks, which had limited effectiveness. This situation, however, was to change by June 1944, paving the way for history's largest carrier battle.

The *Independence*-class new light carrier *Cowpens* (CVL-25) operates with Grumman F6F-3 Hellcats and TBF-1 Avengers on the deck, November 15, 1943. The new fast carrier *Yorktown* (CV-10) is seen in the distance. (National Archives)

Carriers Versus Battleships

The year 1942 began in Europe with German and Italian armies in triumph. At sea the German Navy's submarines were having successes in what their commanders would call the "second happy time" (the first having been from July to October 1941). The Royal Navy was still staggering from the losses of late 1941: the battleship *Barnham* and aircraft carrier *Ark Royal* had been sunk by U-boats in Novemer and the *Repulse* and *Prince of Wales* by Japanese aircraft in December.

After the loss of the *Bismarck* in May 1941 the Germans curtailed surface warship operations in the Atlantic. But there was still a German battle fleet. The battle cruisers *Gneisenau* and *Scharnhorst* were at the French port of Brest, along with the heavy cruiser *Rrinz Eugen*. (Land-based RAF aircraft were unable to destroy those ships while in port or when they escaped up the English Channel to safety in Germany.) In northern waters were the new battleship *Tirpitz* and other warships. Thus, beyond the U-boats, the Germans still had a significant surface force with which to threaten Allied shipping in the Atlantic. In the Mediterranean the Italian fleet, although bloodied, also remained a significant threat while German aircraft poised the major threat to British warships and merchantmen. The Royal Navy would have to be prepared for a breakout of German warships onto the Atlantic.

The hard-pressed Royal Navy also had to send warships—including aircraft carriers—into the Pacific, to deter Japanese advances toward Ceylon and India.

But with entry of the United States into the war, there were some reinforcements for the British fleet. When the war against Japan began in December 1941, there were five U.S. carriers in the Atlantic: the brand-new *Hornet*, the *Ranger*, *Yorktown*, and *Wasp*, plus the first U.S. escort carrier, the *Long Island*, a merchant ship converted to an AVG/CVE in 1941. The *Yorktown* immediately departed for the Pacific, followed in March by the *Hornet*. The *Long Island* was employed mainly as a training ship until she, too, shifted to the Pacific (where she ferried planes to Guadalcanal).

Even before U.S. entry into the war, the *Ranger* and *Wasp* were performing "neutrality patrols" in support of the British. Of the large British carriers, the *Illustrious* and *Formidable* were in U.S. shipyards, the *Victorious* was in the Home Fleet to help guard against a German breakout, and the new *Indomitable* in the Pacific, so the British had no large carriers for

operations in the Mediterranean. The small, outdated *Argus* and *Eagle* were used frequently to carry fighters into the Mediterranean to be flown off for Malta, but their capacity was small and their vulnerability to air and surface attack was great.

In April 1942 the *Wasp*, which had been operating with the British Home Fleet, became the first U.S. carrier to enter the Mediterranean, steaming through the Strait of Gibraltar on April 19 with 47 RAF Spitfires on her deck. Most of her planes were on the hangar deck (some had been flown ashore in Scotland). The following day, after launching 11 of her own F4F Wildcats to fly combat air patrol, the *Wasp* successfully launched the "Spits" for Malta. There were no attacks against the U.S. ship, and she repeated the mission into the Mediterranean in early May with another 47 Spitfires. Again there was no opposition to the ship from German aircraft or Italian ships. The *Wasp* returned to Scotland to pick up the planes she had sent ashore and departed for the United States and, through the Panama Canal, for the war in the Pacific. (At the same time, the *Ranger* carried U.S. Army P-40E fighters across the Atlantic to the African Gold Coast, to be flown across Africa to India and China.)

Large carriers returned to the Mediterranean in August 1942 when four flattops entered the Med—the *Indomitable* and *Victorious*, as well as the amaller *Eagle* with naval aircraft on board and the *Furious* ferrying 38 Spitfires for Malta. In addition to the fighters for Malta, the force was escorting merchant ships. U-boats and German aircraft continually harassed the carriers. The *Eagel* was sunk in just eight minutes after four torpedoes from a U-boat smashed into her. About 250 crewmen died but some 900 were rescued. Air attacks continued, and both the *Indomitable* and *Victorious* were struck by German bombs, but only the *Indomitable*—hit by three bombs—suffered major damage.

Although the British had been fighting the Italians and Germans in North Africa for several years, the entry of the United States permitted a major offensive, and in November 1941 Anglo-American forces invaded French North Africa. The British carriers *Formidable*, *Victorious*, *Furious Argus*, and three escort carriers, as well as the U.S. carrier *Ranger* plus four escort carriers—the largest carrier concentration in the Atlantic theater—supported the landing. On their decks were 353 naval aircraft and 78 U.S. Army P-40F fighters and three observation planes that would be flown ashore when bases were captured.

The landings took place at several points with the carriers providing air support. At Casablanca coastal guns manned by the Vichy French and the 38 cm (15 in) guns of the immobilized battleship *Jean Bart* fired at the Anglo-American invasion fleet. A U.S. battleship returned the French fire; severe damage was inflicted on the anchored French ships before the guns

The HMS *Eagle* launches Sea Hurricanes of No. 801 Squadron for fighter patrol during the Malta convoy operation in the western Mediterranean. (Imperial War Museum)

Battleship *Tirpitz* (*Bismarck* class)
Dates of commissioning and fate: Feb. 25, 1941 / Nov. 12, 1944

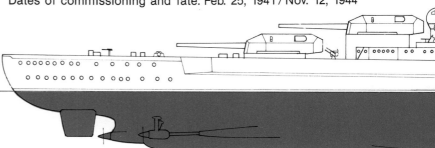

ceased firing. Next, a sortie by French destroyers and submarines was met by fire from U.S. ships and attacks by *Ranger* aircraft. The French were driven back with several ships sunk. The main damage was inflicted by U.S. battleship and cruiser guns, but the *Ranger's* F4F Wildcats and SBD Dauntlesses did their part. This was the only time the *Ranger*, the least capable U.S. carrier, would send her planes against major warships. (A French submarine made an attack on one of the U.S. carriers, probably the *Ranger*, on the 10th but missed.)

North Africa fell to the Allies in May 1943. Three months later Sicily was invaded, with the support of British carriers. During these landings the carrier *Indomitable* was struck on the night of July 15–16 by an Italian aerial torpedo—one of the few successes of the Italian Air Force against British warships. The *Ranger* also operated in the Mediterranean, and a U.S. LST-type landing ship was fitted with a flight deck to fly off observation planes. (Other LSTs would be similarly fitted and for later invasions in the Pacific LSTs would have wire catapult devices for launching light observation planes, which would operate ashore as artillery spotters.)

U.S. and British escort carriers continued to sail the Med, providing support for the landings in Italy from September 1943 and in southern France from August 1944. The larger carriers were needed elsewhere.

In the Altantic, beginning in 1942, the British and U.S. navies increasingly employed escort or "jeep" carriers for convoy escort and as the core of ASW hunter-killer groups. They were also employed in protecting merchant ships on the so-called "Murmansk run," the convoy route from British ports, through the Norwegian Sea, around North Cape, and into the port of Murmansk. The merchant ships were vulnerable to attacks by German land-based bombers and U-boats. And, there was the continued threat from German surface warships.

The greatest threat was the *Tirpitz*, the largest warship to be built by Germany with a displacement of 42,900 tons, carrying eight 38 cm (15 in) guns. Based on the Norwegian coast, the *Tirpitz* threatened to break out into the Atlantic or to attack convoys en route to Murmansk. Since the battleship was completed in the winter of 1941–1942, the RAF had periodically attempted to bomb the ship in Norwegian waters but without effect.

In early March 1942 the *Tirpitz* had gone to sea, with three destroyers, to intercept a convoy in the Norwegian Sea. The British carrier *Victorious*, two battleships, and a battle cruiser were sent to stop the *Tirpitz*. Bad weather prevented the *Victorious* from flying off search planes, and the same fog protected the convoy from the German ships. The weather cleared early on March 9. The *Victorious* flew off a search of six Albacores followed by a dozen Albacores armed with torpedoes.

At 8 a.m. a search plane found the *Tirpitz* and guided in the torpedo bombers. The *Tirpitz* steamed into the wind, forcing the Albacores to make a stern attack at a slow closing speed. There was intensive anti-aircraft fire, and none of the torpedoes hit while two planes were shot down. The *Tirpitz* returned safely to port.

The *Ranger* took up the "Tirpitz" watch with the British Home Fleet in the summer of 1943, when the only large British carrier available in home waters was the outdated *Furious*, and she was undergoing a refit.

The *Tirpitz* remained a threat, although only once in her brief career did she fire her main guns in anger, on that occasion against a British and Norwegian base on the arctic island of Spitzbergen. But her threat to convoys was considerable, especially if the weather prevented British carrier planes from flying. In September 1943 several British midget submarines attacked the *Tirpitz* at anchor in a Norwegian fiord; the X-craft damaged the battleship, putting her out of action for six months. The following month the *Ranger* joined with British ships in attacking German shipping in Norwegian ports, but no effort was made against the disabled German dreadnought.

As repairs to the *Tirpitz* neared completion in early a massive carrier strike was undertaken by the British. The large carriers *Furious* and *Victorious* each carried 21 of the new Barracuda torpedo bombers (cited by some observers as the ugliest plane of the war). These planes would carry 1,600 lb (726 kg) and 500 lb (227 kg) bombs, as the mountains around the fiords would prevent torpedo attacks. There would be escorting fighters from the two large carriers plus four escort carriers. Additional fighters would provide protection for the ships from German bombers.

At 4:15 a.m. on April 3, 1944, the first strike of 21 Barracudas was flown off, and an hour later 19 more bombers were launched; 81 naval Hellcats and Wildcats accompanied them.

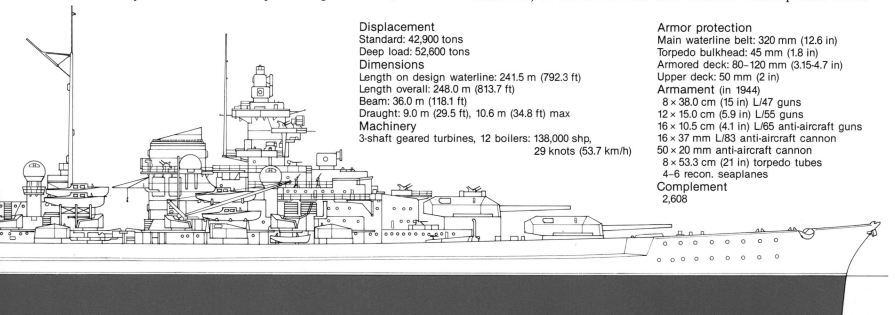

Displacement
Standard: 42,900 tons
Deep load: 52,600 tons
Dimensions
Length on design waterline: 241.5 m (792.3 ft)
Length overall: 248.0 m (813.7 ft)
Beam: 36.0 m (118.1 ft)
Draught: 9.0 m (29.5 ft), 10.6 m (34.8 ft) max
Machinery
3-shaft geared turbines, 12 boilers: 138,000 shp,
29 knots (53.7 km/h)

Armor protection
Main waterline belt: 320 mm (12.6 in)
Torpedo bulkhead: 45 mm (1.8 in)
Armored deck: 80–120 mm (3.15-4.7 in)
Upper deck: 50 mm (2 in)
Armament (in 1944)
8 × 38.0 cm (15 in) L/47 guns
12 × 15.0 cm (5.9 in) L/55 guns
16 × 10.5 cm (4.1 in) L/65 anti-aircraft guns
16 × 37 mm L/83 anti-aircraft cannon
50 × 20 mm anti-aircraft cannon
8 × 53.3 cm (21 in) torpedo tubes
4-6 recon. seaplanes
Complement
2,608

Operation "Mascot" on July 17, 1944. No. 830 Squadron's Fairey Barracuda Mk II torpedo/dive-bomber, armed with a 1,600 lb (726 kg) bomb, takes off from the *Furious* for the strike on the *Tirpitz*. (Imperial War Museum)

The flight of 120 miles (220 km) was made without incident, and there was no anti-aircraft fire over the fiord until the first bombs were released. The *Tirpitz* suffered 14 direct hits plus one damaging near miss. The larger, armor-piercing bombs, however, were released so low that none penetrated the battleship's massive deck armor, and one even failed to explode. Still the ship's superstructure was devastated, and 122 men were killed and more than 300 were wounded. The *Tirpitz* was out of action for another three months. The attack cost the British two bombers and a fighter in combat, plus a Barracuda that crashed on takeoff.

During April and May 1944 these carriers made anti-shipping strikes along the Norwegian coast. They attempted another raid against the *Tirpitz* on April 24, but that operation was cancelled because of bad weather. On May 14 the *Furious* and *Victorious* flew off 27 Barracudas escorted by 36 fighters to attack the *Tirpitz*, but this raid was also aborted because of bad weather. There was a need to sink the *Tirpitz* to free the large carriers for the campaign in the Pacific.

On July 17, 1944, the *Formidable*, *Furious*, and the recently completed *Indefatigable* launched a raid of 44 Barracudas against the *Tirpitz* with an escort of 48 fighters. This time the Germans had sufficient warning of the strike to cover the fiord with smoke, obscuring the battleship. None of the bombs struck the ship, and a second strike was frustrated by fog. Two planes were lost in this effort.

Still another carrier raid was attempted in late August.

The damaged *Tirpitz* surrounded by torpedo nets in Kaafjord, the northern tip of Norway, in July 1944. (Imperial War Museum)

This sixth carrier raid consisted of the *Formidable*, *Furious*, *Indefatigable*, and a pair of escort carriers. On the morning of August 22 the ships sent off 31 Barracudas and 53 fighters, but they were turned back by fog. That evening an effort was made by six bomb-carrying Hellcats to reach the *Tirpitz*; they inflicted no damage. Two days later the carriers were back. This time the three large carriers launched 33 Barracudas and 44 fighters, some of the latter being American-built Corsairs carrying 1,000 lb (454 kg) bombs. The planes bombed through the smokescreen, and the Barracudas hit with one 1,600 lb (726 kg) bomb and the Corsairs with one 1,000 lb (454 kg) bomb. The larger bomb failed to explode, and the smaller hit atop a heavily armored main turret. No damage was inflicted while six planes were lost.

The *Formidable* and *Indefatigable* struck again on August 29. (The *Furious* had returned to port and was soon placed in reserve, ending her very active 27-year naval career.) There were 26 Barracudas plus 41 fighters this time; again there was a smokescreen and intensive anti-aircraft fire waiting for the attackers. No bombs hit the *Tirpitz* and two aircraft were lost. Within the period of a week three fleet carriers and two escort carriers had flown off 242 sorties against an anchored battleship and were unable to inflict significant damage. This was perhaps the most striking failure of carrier aviation in World War II and can be directly attributed to the lack of adequate British aircraft—the Barracuda was too slow and its bomb load too small to be effective.

The RAF then began flying raids against the *Tirpitz* with four-engine Lancaster bombers. On November 12 the bombers scored three hits and two near misses with 12,000 lb (5,443 kg) bombs. The *Tirpitz* rolled over and sank in the shallow fiord. One Lancaster was lost on the raid.

With the *Tirpitz* sunk the principal mission of carriers in the Atlantic region became the ASW campaign in the Atlantic. But the carriers best suited for the U-boat war were the British and American escort carriers, each with their 15 to 30 fighters and bombers. The large British carriers, armored-deck ships of the *Illustrious* class, were being transferred to the Indian and, subsequently, Pacific Oceans, there to support the Allied ground offensive—and to possibly engage the Japanese fleet.

The Biggest Carrier Battle

On June 6, 1944, as Allied troops stormed ashore on the beaches of Normandy, halfway around the world a massive U.S. fleet steamed from its anchorage at Majuro atoll in the Marshalls and set course for the Marianas. Leading the fleet was a fast carrier force consisting of seven fast carriers and eight light carriers, seven fast battleships, and numerous supporting ships. The armada of transports and landing ships that followed was accompanied by 11 escort carriers to provide close air support for the assault troops.

The fast carriers—with almost 900 aircraft on board—launched strikes to begin the Marianas assault on the afternoon of June 11. The Japanese high command was again taken by surprise. For eight days the virtually unopposed U.S. carrier planes strafed and bombed Japanese positions in the Marianas.

With the first American strikes the alarm was sounded on board Japanese warships at the main fleet base at Tawi Tawi, an island in the Sulu Sea in the southern Philippines. This base was close to the oil fields in Borneo, reducing the need for tankers to run the guantlet of American submarines that were interdicting merchant ships travelling from the East Indies to Japan. The Japanese fleet made preparaitons for going to sea.

U.S. submarines were keeping close watch on Tawi Tawi, and even before the Japanese ships went to sea the submarines sank four destroyers and three of the invaluable oilers. On June 13 the First Mobile Fleet sortied (and was immediately reported by a watching U.S. submarine). There were nine aircraft carriers in the First Mobile Fleet: the war-tested veterans *Shokaku* and *Zuikaku*; the brand-new *Taiho* (52 aircraft); the

Hiyo and *Junyo*, both 24,140-ton converted passenger liners (48 aircraft); the former seaplane carriers *Chitose* and *Chiyoda*, converted to 11,190-ton light carriers; and the veteran CVLs *Ryuho* and *Zuiho*. These nine ships carried about 440 aircraft. Three battleships and a screen of cruisers and destroyers escorted the Japanese carriers.

The two carrier fleets steaming for the largest carrier battle were thus badly matched: the U.S. force had 15 carriers with almost 900 aircraft; the Japanese force had nine carriers but only 440 aircraft. Further, the U.S. pilots were well trained—most with combat experience—compared to the Japanese fliers, most of whom were poorly trained, in part because of the severe fuel shortages and threat of U.S. submarines that had stopped the carriers from exercising at sea and restricted the pilots flying from airfields ashore.

The Japanese planes, however, had a greater search and attack range than the U.S. planes (due to their lack of armor and self-sealing fuel tanks), and the battle would be fought within range of land-based Japanese aircraft in the Marianas, permitting Japanese carrier planes to use the Marianas bases. In the easterly tradewinds the Japanese could launch and recover planes while approaching the U.S. forces, while the U.S. carriers would have to steam away from the enemy during flight operations.

There was one other factor: the American submarines. They tracked and reported on the Japanese force as it steamed north, through the Sulu Sea and the Philippines, passing between Luzon and Samar on the afternoon of June 15 and entering the Philippine Sea. That same day U.S. Marines landed on Saipan. Later that day two battleships and additional cruisers and destroyers joined the Japanese force.

Grumman F6F-3 Hellcats of VF-15, Commander David S. McCampbell in the lead, running up before a sweep over Marianas from the *Essex* in mid-June 1944. Wings-folded Curtiss SB2C-1C Helldivers of VB-15 are seen at the back of the fighters. (National Archives)

Type 0 Mk 52 fighters (A6M5s) and Type 0 Mk 21 fighter-bombers (modified A6M2s) prepare for launch from the *Chiyoda* on June 19, 1944, during the Battle of the Philippine Sea. (Yoji Watanabe)

On June 18 the Japanese launched large-scale searches with carrier planes and floatplanes from cruisers. They would not fail to locate the American carriers as they had at Midway. Sighting reports of the American carriers began coming in just after 3 p.m. But the distance—over 400 miles (740 km)—would mean that planes sent out to strike them would have to land back on board the carriers at night, too difficult a task for the inexperienced Japanese pilots. Accordingly, the Japanese ships reversed and steamed slowly westward, making preparations to launch attacks at dawn the next morning.

At the same time, the U.S. carrier force commander urged that his carriers steam westward during the night to similarly launch early on the 19th. While U.S. submarines had tracked the Japanese warships, they had not been able to specifically identify the aircraft carriers. Further, U.S. scout planes had not located the Japanese carriers. The U.S. fleet commander, believing that, as at Midway and in the Solomons battles, the Japanese could be in separate forces and that his carriers might be decoyed, decided to "play it safe" and keep the fast carriers close to the Saipan beachhead.

At 1:15 a.m. on June 19 a PBM Mariner flying boat made radar contact with the First Mobile Fleet—the largest concentration of Japanese warships in the entire war. Forty ships in two groups appeared on the PBM's radarscope. Communications difficulties and the failure of other units to relay its sighting reports delayed this news from reaching the fleet commanders for seven and a half hours. An hour later the U.S. carriers began launching a search of 15 radar-equipped Avengers. These were followed at dawn by more scout planes.

At about this time several Japanese aircraft appeared on carrier radarscopes coming from the *east*, from the heavily bombed runways on the island of Guam. These planes were easily chased away by carrier-based F6F Hellcats. During the morning more and more Japanese planes approached the force, apparently being flown up from Japanese bases to the south. As a result, scores of Hellcats were now airborne. The result was 30 Japanese fighters and five bombers shot down at the cost of one Hellcat. Still more planes were being detected when, at one minute past ten o'clock, all U.S. fighters were ordered to break off action and return to the task force.

History's largest carrier battle was already beginning. The First Mobile Fleet commenced launching aircraft at 4:45 a.m. on June 19, an hour and a half before sunrise. First floatplanes were catapulted from battleships and cruisers to seek out the American carriers. These were followed at intervals by more scout planes, including Kates, D4Y Judy (*Suisei*) dive bombers and B6N Jill (*Tenzan*) torpedo bombers from the carriers. In all 44 Japanese planes were searching for the American ships.

At 7:30 a.m. the Japanese commanders received the first reports of American carriers from their scout planes dispatched earlier. After additional reports, an hour later the first Japanese strike of 64 aircraft was launched. These were followed by another strike of 128 aircraft. Eight of these planes developed engine trouble and returned to their ships, while two planes were shot down when they were fired on by *Japanese* ships as they passed over. In addition, one Japanese pilot sighted a torpedo streaking toward the carrier *Taiho* as he took off. He made a suicide dive on the torpedo and exploded it.

A third strike was launched with 49 aircraft and, before noon, a fourth strike of 83 planes was flown off. Three hundred and thirteen aircraft were en route to strike the American carriers.

But the first attack of the carrier battle was made by a U.S. submarine. The undersea craft had found the Japanese carriers and fired a six-torpedo spread at the new, 29,300 ton *Taiho*. One torpedo was exploded by the sacrifice of the *Taiho* pilot; four torpedoes missed the carrier. One hit. That torpedo exploded, jamming one of the ship's elevators and causing leaks in the fuel oil, gasoline, and water systems. There was no fire and flight operations were unhindered. At 29,300 tons the *Taiho* was the largest aircraft carrier in service except for the USS *Saratoga*, but with steam turbines and not the tricky turbo-electric drive of the "Sara," it would take much more than a single torpedo to stop the *Taiho*...or so it was thought.

Shortly before 11 a.m. the first Japanese strike aircraft sighted the U.S. carrier force. The 15 carriers had put up most of their 450 F6F Hellcats. Their bombers had been flown off—some to bomb the runways on Guam—to keep the decks clear for the fighters to land, refuel, and go aloft again. The Hellcats

A near miss on the *Bunker Hill*, June 19, 1944. The photograph was taken from the light carrier *Monterey*. (National Archives)

were guided to the approaching Japanese planes by directors in the carriers who used radar bearings to control the intercepts. Beyond the Hellcats were the massive anti-aircraft batteries of the carriers, battleships, cruisers, and destroyers.

The first wave of 64 attackers ran into waves of Hellcats. The mêlée was brief. Forty-one of the Japanese planes were shot down. One U.S. fighter was shot down (its pilot rescued). This raid scored a single bomb hit on a battleship and another crashed into a second dreadnought. There was some damage and 27 dead on the first ship; there was essentially no damage to the second.

Then came the surviving 117 aircraft of the second Japanese strike. The Hellcats and anti-aircraft fire destroyed 94 of these aircraft. The only damage they caused was minor, from near bomb misses of the carriers.

Of the third, 49-plane strike, several became lost and returned to their carriers. Of the planes that found U.S. ships, seven were shot down, but the survivors inflicted no damage. The fourth, 83-plane raid entirely missed the U.S. carriers, and many headed for airfields on Rota and Guam. Before reaching the runways they encountered swarms of F6F Hellcats. A few did sight some American ships but were splashed by anti-aircraft fire. In all, at least 55 planes from this fourth raid were destroyed before they could land.

By 3 p.m. the skies over the U.S. carrier force were empty of Japanese planes. Over 200 attacking planes had been shot down—two by Japanese anti-aircraft fire, the rest by U.S. Hellcats and anti-aircraft guns. Another 22 scout planes were lost. There were a few operational losses. In all, some 230 aircraft were lost. Adding the 50 or so land-based planes from the Marianas that were shot down, and 22 planes lost later in the day on board carriers that sank, the Japanese losses were over 300 planes on June 19.

In stark contrast, the U.S. carrier force suffered 23 planes shot down and six more that crashed operationally. (In addition to the 27 fliers in those planes, 31 Americans were killed on board ship.) There was no appreciable damage to U.S. ships from these massive air attacks. The destruction of Japanese aircraft on June 19 was quickly named the "Marianas Turkey Shoot."

As the aerial battle was being fought over the U.S. carriers and the Marianas, some 200 miles (370 km) away the First Mobile Fleet was suffering its first losses although the U.S. carriers had not yet launched a strike. The damage from the torpedo hit on the *Taiho* was being repaired when just after noon another U.S. submarine fired a salvo of six torpedoes at the *Shokaku*. Three hit. Her fuel tanks ruptured, and the *Shokaku* burst into flame. She fell out of formation, and shortly after 3 p.m. the ship blew up and sank. Her casualties were heavy—1,263 men died with the veteran carrier. A short time later the escaping gasoline fumes in the *Taiho* caused an explosion that devastated the carrier. She sank with some 1,500 of her crew.

The Japanese still had seven carriers with 102 aircraft on their decks. The First Mobile Fleet turned northwest, to reorganize, refuel, and prepare for the resumption of battle on June 21. Meanwhile, several hundred miles to the east, 12 of the U.S. carriers set course in pursuit of the Japanese warships. Three carriers and their consorts would remain off the Marianas, refuel, and take up the pursuit on the 21st. During the night radar-equipped carrier fighters orbited over Rota and Guam and at dawn the parting carriers sent a fighter sweep over Guam.

On the afternoon of June 20 the U.S. carrier search planes had at last located the Japanese carriers, which had not been seen since the PBM sightings of the previous morning. After brief consideration, the U.S. carrier force commander ordered every available strike plane into the air, realizing that they would have to be recovered after dark. The carriers that were already in pursuit of the Japanese began launching aircraft at 4:21 p.m. Within ten minutes 11 of the carriers launched 216 aircraft—85 Hellcat fighters, 54 TBF/TBM Avenger torpedo planes, and 77 dive bombers. The last were mostly SB2C Helldivers, which were now replacing the outstanding SBD Dauntless. Although the SB2C was newer and had superior performance, the Dauntless was better liked by Navy pilots and in general performed better than its successor.

These planes were launched 220 miles (410 km) from the reported Japanese carrier position. A short time later came reports that the Japanese were actually 60 miles (110 km) farther away. Because the U.S. flattops had to steam eastward to launch

The 1st Air Flotilla including the *Zuikaku*, the main division of the First Mobile Fleet, maneuvers under air attack on June 20, 1944. (National Archives)

aircraft, the distance between the two fleets was closer to 300 miles (560 km)

Shortly before sundown the U.S. planes sighted the Japanese ships. First seen was an oiler group then, farther off, the three carrier groups. Zeros climbed skyward to intercept the attackers. But the Hellcats pushed them aside, clearing the way for the dive bombers and torpedo planes. The oilers were the first targets; three were damaged, two of them so badly that they had to be sunk. Next the U.S. planes attacked the carriers.

Avengers put two torpedoes into the *Hiyo*. The 24,140-ton ship erupted in flame and began to sink. Her sister ship *Junyo* was hit by two bombs and shaken by near misses, but shie survived. The attackers then concentrated on the *Zuikaku*; she took a single bomb hit and several near misses; she would survive the battle. Finally, the carrier *Chiyoda* suffered a bomb hit and some other ships were damaged.

Now the American fliers faced the ordeal of the long, night flight back to their carriers. The U.S. ships were steaming westward at 22 knots to close the distance; still, the carrier planes had a return flight of 240 to 300 miles (445 to 560 km). At 10:45 the first planes arrived over the darkened carriers. A few radar-equipped night fighters (F6F-3N) were sent aloft to guide the planes. On his flagship *Lexington* the task force commander ordered: "Turn on the lights." The carriers and thier screening ships turned on their searchlights and pointed them skyward.

Although Japanese submarines had not been detected, they might have been present. A more significant threat would have been night attackers from the Japanese carriers or from the airfields on Guam. The searchlights provided beacons for the carriers that could be used by friend or foe. But the searchlights saved hundreds of carrier pilots. The planes came down on the carriers, many running out of fuel as they touched the flight decks. Pilots didn't care which carrier they found, any flight deck that was not clogged was acceptable. Some planes ignored wave off signals, and there were some deck crashes. Many planes could not reach a flight deck before fuel was exhausted and they came down into the water.

One hundred of the 216 aircraft sent on the strike were lost. Twenty aircraft were shot down over the Japanese fleet; 80 planes were lost in deck crashes, pushed over the side to make space for planes to land, or came down at sea when they ran out of fuel. More than half of the SB2Cs that were launched on the raid came down at sea. The losses in pilots and crewmen was relatively small—49 men died that aftetnoon of 401 who flew on the strike.

By 11 p.m. the last plane was recovered or had crashed at sea. The American ships, which had turned eastward for the recovery, again swung their bows to the west in pursuit of the Japanese carriers. There were still six carriers in the Japanese force. There were, however, only 34 carrier aircraft available, and there would be no Japanese strikes on the 22nd.

During the night the PBM flying boats and Avengers with radar carried out long-range searches. More carrier scout planes followed in the morning. The Japanese ships were found 360 miles (670 km) from the carriers, too far for an effective strike. The fifth and largest carrier-versus-carrier battle of the war was over.

Despite the large number of Japanese carriers and aircraft that sailed into battle, they were outnumbered by the U.S. force, which had the advantages of submarines to track and attack the Japanese ships, superior aircraft, and superior pilots. The outcome of the Battle of the Philippine Sea was never really in doubt. The Marianas campaign continued until August 10, when the former U.S. island of Guam was recaptured. There was never another threat from the Japanese fleet. The campaign had cost the Japanese more than 1,200 aircraft destroyed with three carriers sunk—one lost to U.S. carrier aircraft and two to submarines. Several other ships were damaged.

No major U.S. ships sustained serious damage in the Marianas campaign. No U.S. ships larger than landing craft were sunk. In two months of combat the 15 fast carriers had lost 358 aircraft to all causes; most of their crews were recovered.

The Battle of the Marianas marked the end of the Japanese carriers as an effective fighting force.

Nakajima carrier-based torpedo-bomber
Tenzan Mk 11 (B6N1, Allied code name: Jill)
of the 601st *Kokutai* based aboard
the *Zuikaku* in early 1944.

Power unit
Nakajima *Mamori* Mk 11 14-cylinder air-cooled engine
: 1,870 hp for take-off
 1,600 hp at 4,900 m (16,080 ft)
Dimensions
Span: 14.895 m (48 ft 10$^{7/16}$ in)
Span folded: 7.195 m (23 ft 7$^{1/4}$ in)
Length, tail up: 10.735 m (35 ft 2$^{5/8}$ in)
Height, tail up: 4.302 m (14 ft 1$^{3/8}$ in)
Wing area: 37.2 m² (400.4 sq ft)
Weights
Empty: 3,223 kg (7,105 lb)
Normal gross: 5,200 kg (11,460 lb)
Performance
Max speed: 465 km/h (289 mph) at 4,800 m (15,750 ft)
Cruising speed: 333 km/h (207 mph) at 4,000 m (13,120 ft)
Time to climb to 3,000 m (9,840 ft): 5 min 54 sec
Normal range: 1,463 km (909 mls)
Overloaded range: 2,698 km (1,677 mls)
Armament
Torpedo: 1 × 800 kg (1,764 lb)
Bombs: 1 × 800 kg (1,764 lb) or 2 × 250 kg (551 lb)
        or 6 × 60 kg (132 lb)
Flexible mounted aft-firing: 1 × 7.7 mm (0.303 in)
                Type 92 machine gun
Ventral flexible mounted aft-firing: 1 × 7.7 mm (0.303 in)
                Type 92 machine gun

Crew
3

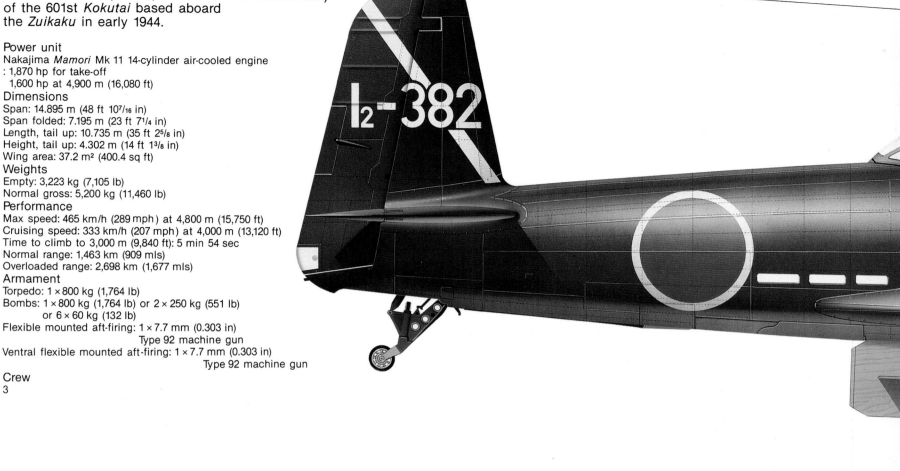

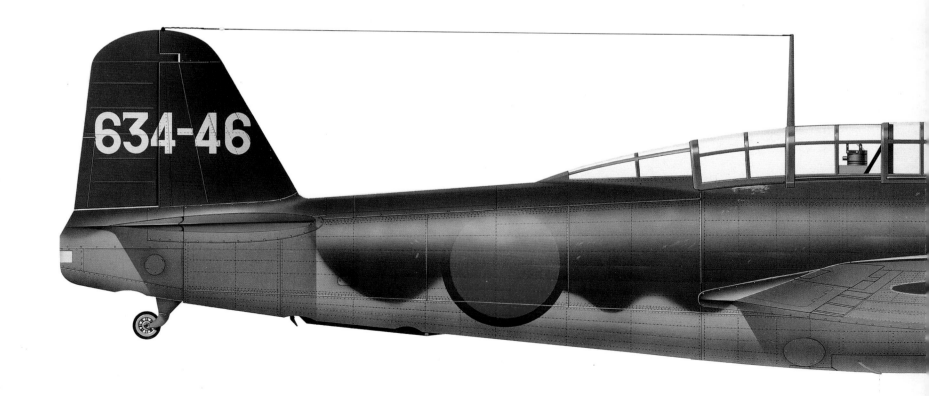

Scale ¹/₂₈

Aircraft Carriers in the Battle of the Philippine Sea (June 19–20, 1944)

U.S. Navy Task Force 58

	Task Group 58.1	Task Group 58.2	Task Group 58.3	Task Group 58.4
Aircraft carriers	CV-12 *Hornet* CV-10 *Yorktown* CVL-24 *Belleau Wood* CVL-29 *Bataan*	CV-17 *Bunker Hill* CV-18 *Wasp* CVL-26 *Monterey* CVL-28 *Cabot*	CV-6 *Enterprise* CV-16 *Lexington* CVL-30 *San Jacinto* CVL-23 *Princeton*	CV-9 *Essex* — CVL-27 *Langley* CVL-25 *Cowpens*
Fighters	127 F6F-3	116 F6F-3	116 F6F-3	84 F6F-3
Night fighters	8 F6F-3N —	8 F6F-3N —	4 F6F-3N 3 F4U-2	4 F6F-3N —
Dive bombers	73 SB2C-1C 4 SBD-5	65 SB2C-1C —	— 55 SBD-5	36 SB2C-1C —
Torpedo planes	53 TBF/TBM-1C	53 TBF/TBM-1C/-1D	49 TBF/TBM-1C/-1D	38 TBF/TBM-1C

Japanese Navy First Mobile Fleet

	The 1st Air Flotilla	The 2nd Air Flotilla	The 3rd Air Flotilla
Aircraft carriers	CV *Taiho* CV *Shokaku* CV *Zuikaku*	CV *Junyo* CV *Hiyo* CVL *Ryuho*	CVL *Chiyoda* CVL *Chitose* CVL *Zuiho*
Fighters	80 A6M5	53 A6M5	18 A6M5
Fighter-bombers	11 A6M2	27 A6M2	45 A6M2
Diver bombers	70 D4Y1/Y1-C 9 D3A2	11 D4Y1 29 D3A2	— —
Torpedo planes	44 B6N2 —	15 B6N2 —	9 B6N2 18 B5N2

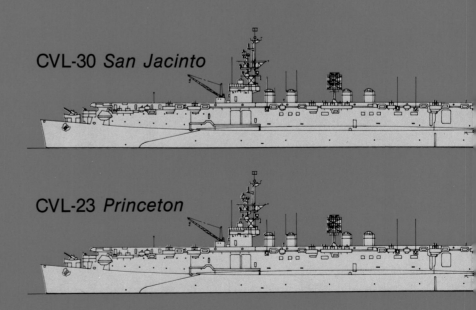

CVL-30 *San Jacinto*

CVL-23 *Princeton*

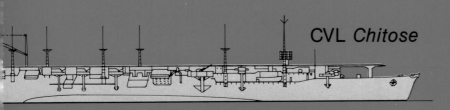

CVL *Chitose*

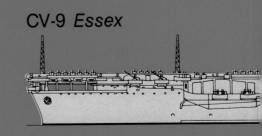

CV-9 *Essex*

The 1st Air Flotilla

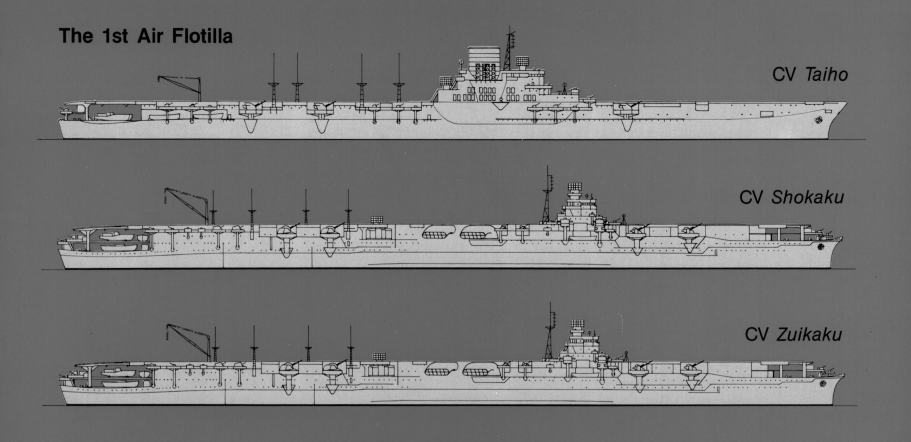

CV *Taiho*

CV *Shokaku*

CV *Zuikaku*

The 2nd Air Flotilla

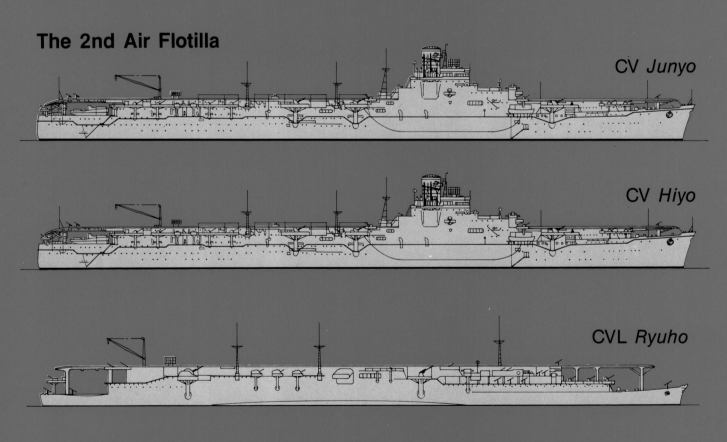

CV *Junyo*

CV *Hiyo*

CVL *Ryuho*

The 3rd Air Flotilla

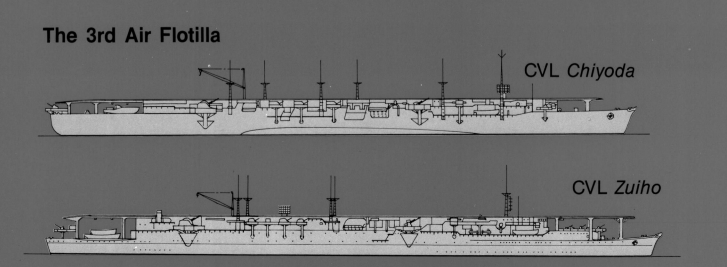

CVL *Chiyoda*

CVL *Zuiho*

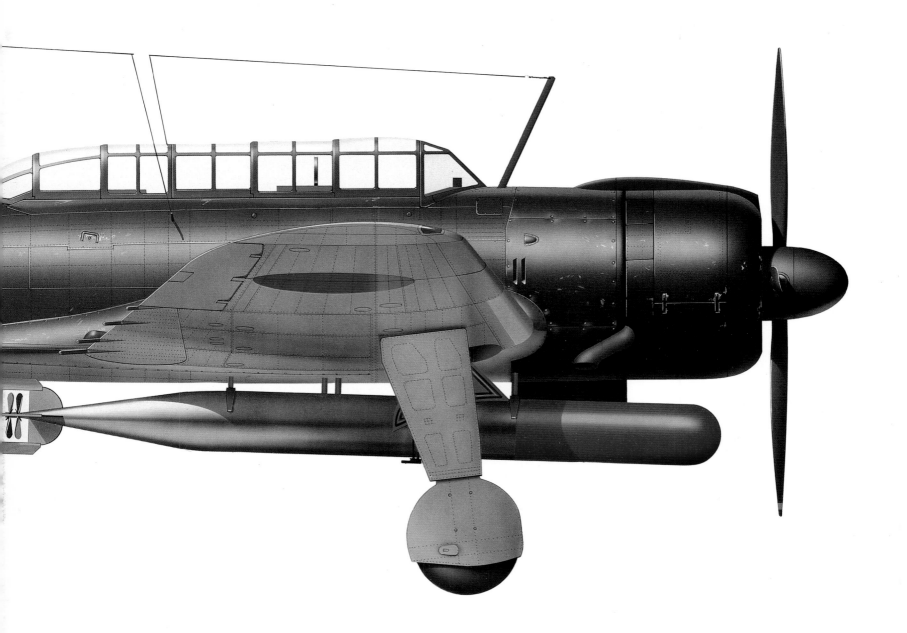

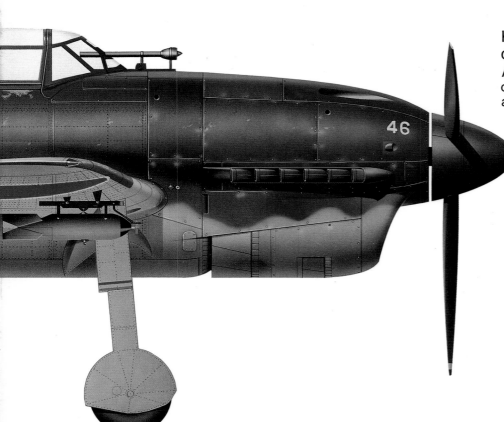

Koku-Gijutsusho (Naval Aero-Technical Arsenal) carrier-based dive-bomber *Suisei* Mk 11 (D4Y1, Allied code name: Judy) late production model of the 634th *Kokutai* based aboard battleship-carriers *Ise* and *Hyuga* (both planned) about the middle of 1944.

Power unit
Aichi *Atsuta* Mk 21 12-cylinder liquid-cooled engine
: 1,200 hp for take-off
   965 hp at 4,450 m (14,600 ft)
Dimensions
Span: 11.50 m (37 ft 8³/₄ in)
Length, tail up: 10.22 m (33 ft 6³/₈ in)
Height, tail up: 3.63 m (11 ft 10¹⁵/₁₆ in)
Wing area: 23.6 m² (254 sq ft)
Weights
Empty: 2,440 kg (5,380 lb)
Normal gross: 3,650 kg (8,050 lb)
Performance
Max speed: 552 km/h (343 mph) at 4,750 m (15,580 ft)
Cruising speed: 426 km/h (265 mph) at 3,000 m (9,840 ft)
Time to climb to 3,000 m (9,840 ft): 5 min 14 sec
Normal range: 1,580 km (982 mls)
Overloaded range: 2,590 km (1,610 mls)
Armament
Bombs: 1 × 500 kg (1,102 lb) and 2 × 60 kg (132 lb)
Fixed forward-firing: 2 × 7.7 mm (0.303 in)
                    Type 97 machine guns
Flexible mounted aft-firing: 1 × 7.7 mm (0.303 in)
                    Type 92 machine gun

Crew
2

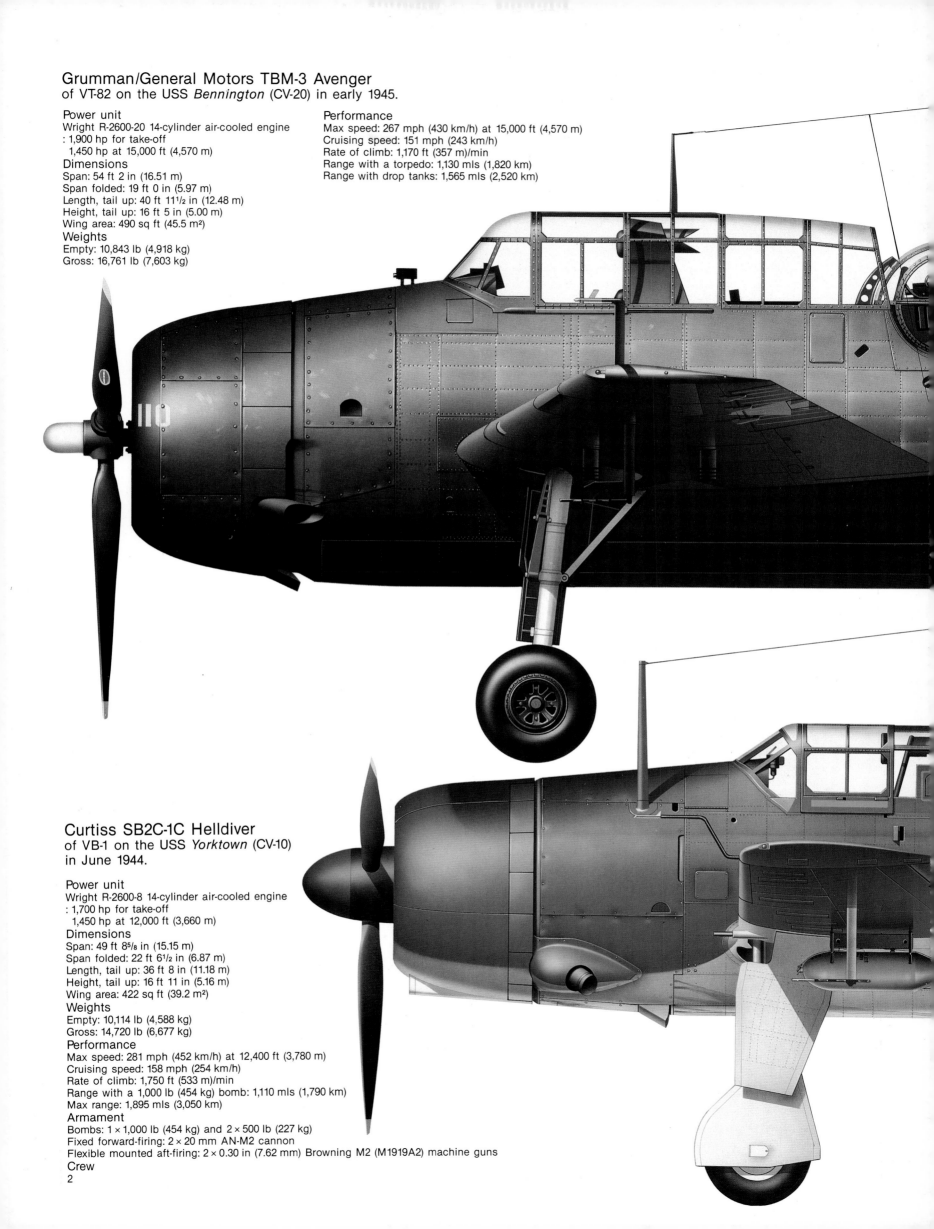

Grumman/General Motors TBM-3 Avenger
of VT-82 on the USS *Bennington* (CV-20) in early 1945.

Power unit
Wright R-2600-20 14-cylinder air-cooled engine
: 1,900 hp for take-off
  1,450 hp at 15,000 ft (4,570 m)
Dimensions
Span: 54 ft 2 in (16.51 m)
Span folded: 19 ft 0 in (5.97 m)
Length, tail up: 40 ft 11½ in (12.48 m)
Height, tail up: 16 ft 5 in (5.00 m)
Wing area: 490 sq ft (45.5 m²)
Weights
Empty: 10,843 lb (4,918 kg)
Gross: 16,761 lb (7,603 kg)

Performance
Max speed: 267 mph (430 km/h) at 15,000 ft (4,570 m)
Cruising speed: 151 mph (243 km/h)
Rate of climb: 1,170 ft (357 m)/min
Range with a torpedo: 1,130 mls (1,820 km)
Range with drop tanks: 1,565 mls (2,520 km)

Curtiss SB2C-1C Helldiver
of VB-1 on the USS *Yorktown* (CV-10) in June 1944.

Power unit
Wright R-2600-8 14-cylinder air-cooled engine
: 1,700 hp for take-off
  1,450 hp at 12,000 ft (3,660 m)
Dimensions
Span: 49 ft 8⅝ in (15.15 m)
Span folded: 22 ft 6½ in (6.87 m)
Length, tail up: 36 ft 8 in (11.18 m)
Height, tail up: 16 ft 11 in (5.16 m)
Wing area: 422 sq ft (39.2 m²)
Weights
Empty: 10,114 lb (4,588 kg)
Gross: 14,720 lb (6,677 kg)
Performance
Max speed: 281 mph (452 km/h) at 12,400 ft (3,780 m)
Cruising speed: 158 mph (254 km/h)
Rate of climb: 1,750 ft (533 m)/min
Range with a 1,000 lb (454 kg) bomb: 1,110 mls (1,790 km)
Max range: 1,895 mls (3,050 km)
Armament
Bombs: 1 × 1,000 lb (454 kg) and 2 × 500 lb (227 kg)
Fixed forward-firing: 2 × 20 mm AN-M2 cannon
Flexible mounted aft-firing: 2 × 0.30 in (7.62 mm) Browning M2 (M1919A2) machine guns
Crew

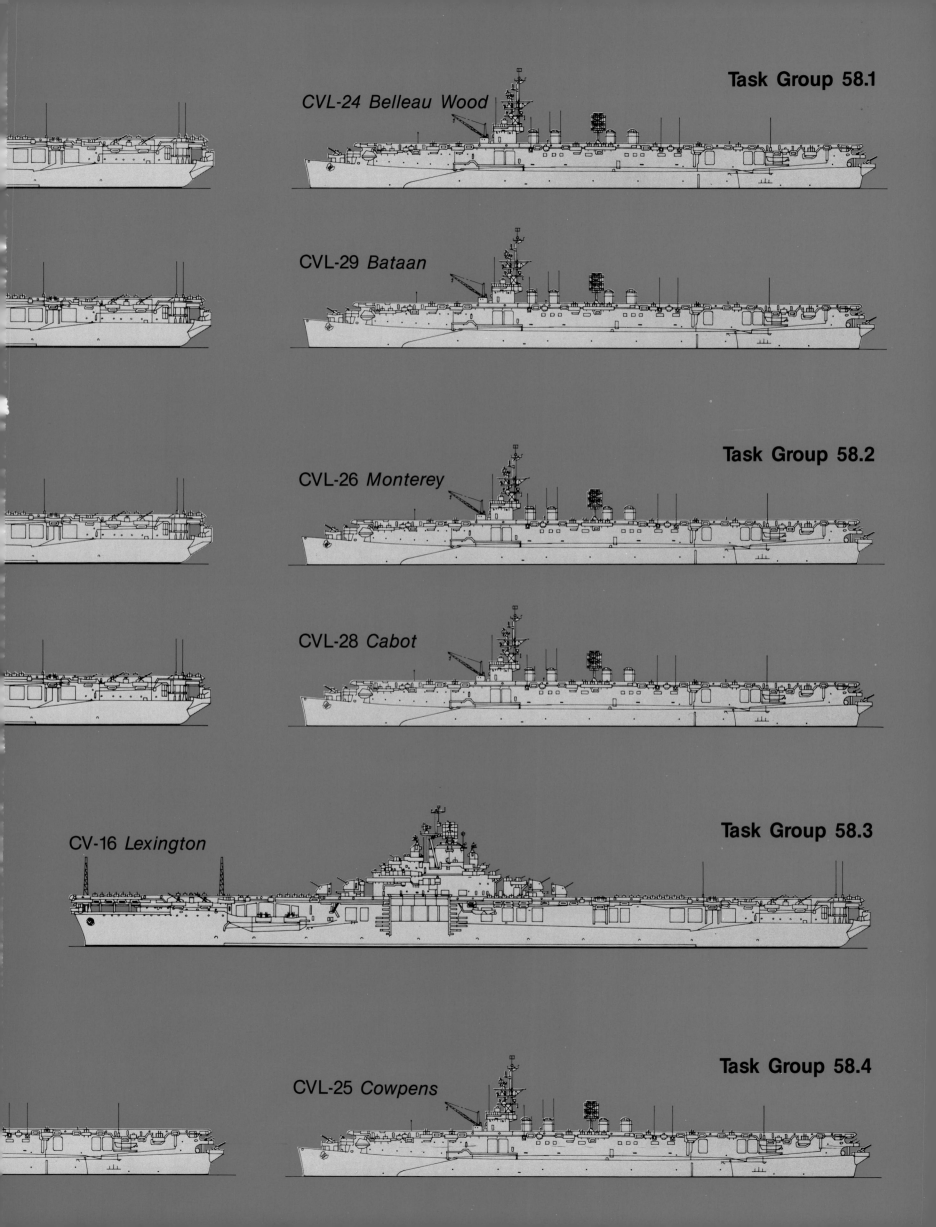

Task Group 58.1

CVL-24 *Belleau Wood*

CVL-29 *Bataan*

Task Group 58.2

CVL-26 *Monterey*

CVL-28 *Cabot*

Task Group 58.3

CV-16 *Lexington*

Task Group 58.4

CVL-25 *Cowpens*

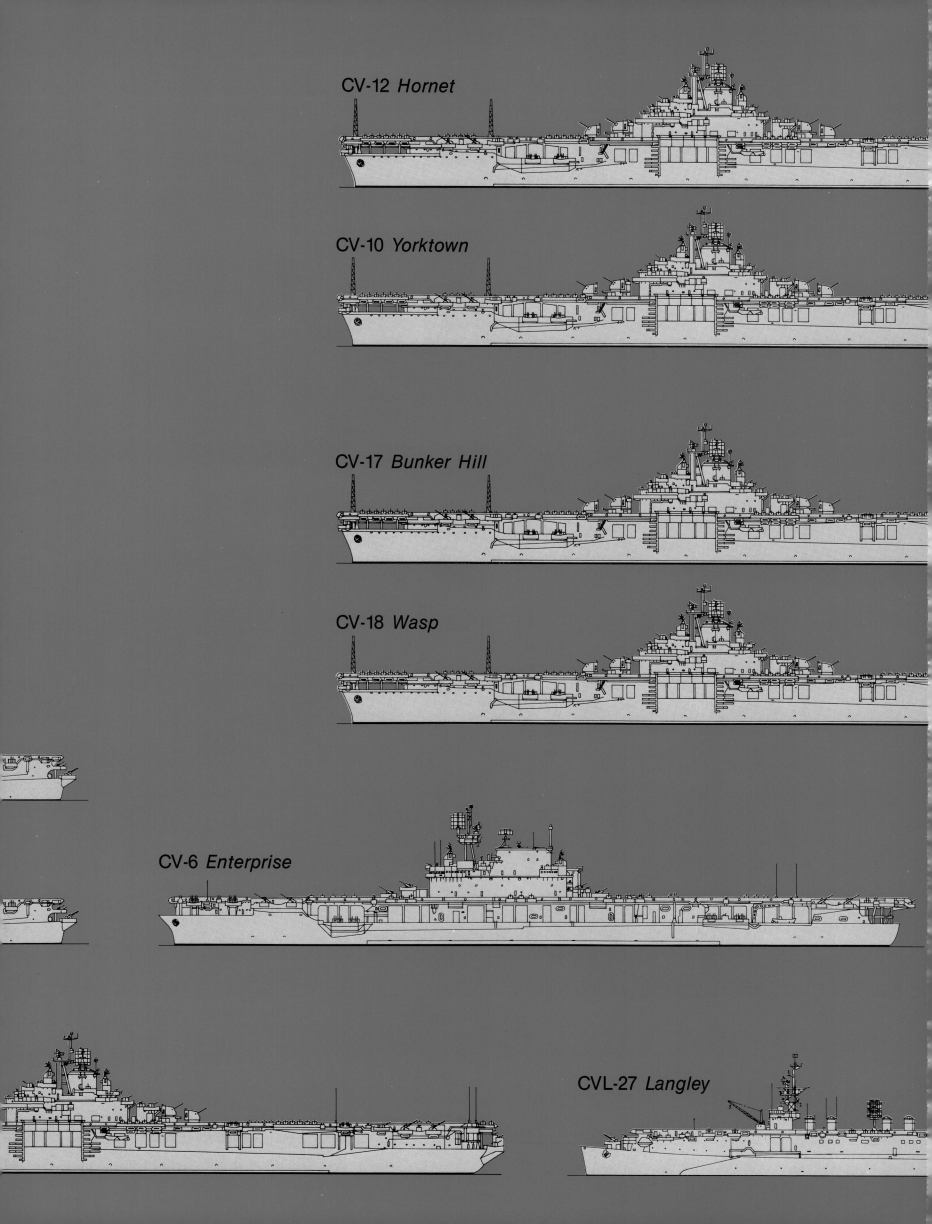

CV-12 *Hornet*

CV-10 *Yorktown*

CV-17 *Bunker Hill*

CV-18 *Wasp*

CV-6 *Enterprise*

CVL-27 *Langley*

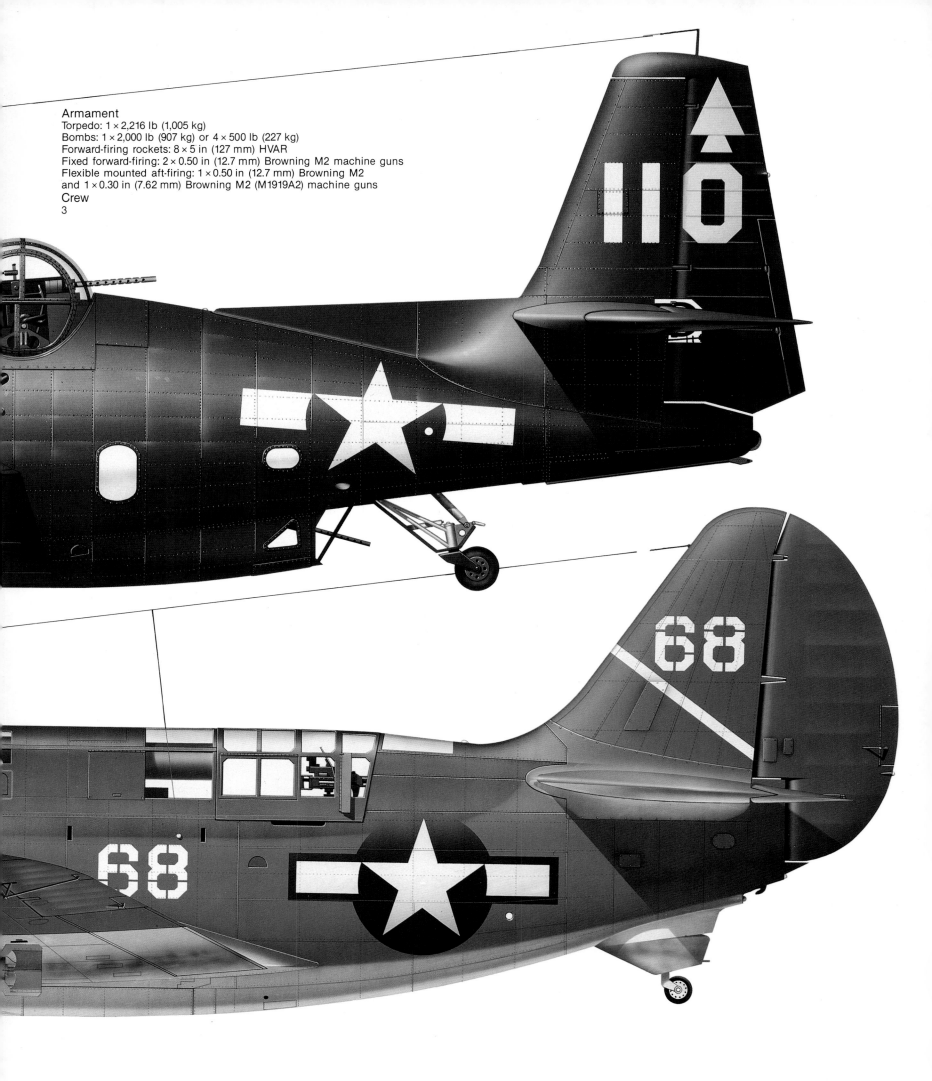

Armament
Torpedo: 1 × 2,216 lb (1,005 kg)
Bombs: 1 × 2,000 lb (907 kg) or 4 × 500 lb (227 kg)
Forward-firing rockets: 8 × 5 in (127 mm) HVAR
Fixed forward-firing: 2 × 0.50 in (12.7 mm) Browning M2 machine guns
Flexible mounted aft-firing: 1 × 0.50 in (12.7 mm) Browning M2
and 1 × 0.30 in (7.62 mm) Browning M2 (M1919A2) machine guns
Crew
3

Scale 1/28

Carrier Victory

The American offensive in the Pacific had followed two widely separated routes in 1943–1944: following the assault on Guadalcanal, U.S. Army troops moved north through the Solomons chain, the Bismarck archipelago, and along the northern coast of New Guinea. The Navy carried the troops and provided gunfire support and defense against Japanese attacks. Land-based aircraft provided most of the support, but periodically the fast carriers entered the area to add their firepower.

At the same time, the Navy-Marine thrust across the Pacific had captured or neutralized the Japanese airfields in the Gilbert and Marshall island groups and in June of 1944 began the recapture of the Marianas.

The next major objective would bring the dual thrusts together in the Philippines. The recapture of the Philippines was begun in September when U.S. fast carriers began a series of strikes against Japanese positions in the island. There were 16 carriers available to the U.S. Fast Carrier Force: seven *Essex*-class ships, the venerable *Enterprise*, and eight *Independence*-class light carriers, with over 1,000 aircraft embarked. Two-thirds of these aircraft were F6F Hellcats, a reflection of the excellence of the plane as a fighter, scouting aircraft, and attack aircraft. The remaining planes were SB2C Helldivers—the not overly popular dive bombers—and TBF/TBM Avenger torpedo planes.

The assault on the Philippines began early on September 9 as the carriers, at their closest point only 50 miles (90 km) off the coast, sent huge fighter sweeps over the southern Philippines. For two days the American planes attacked with impunity, brushing aside the few defending fighters. This success led the carriers to strike farther north, at Luzon with its capital city

of Manila. The fast carriers then provided support to the capture of Peleliu and Ulithi in the Carolines. The latter's broad lagoon would become the principal anchorage for the Pacific Fleet and its staging base for the assault on the Philippines.

For the October invasion the Fast Carrier Force would number nine large and eight light carriers with over 1,200 aircraft! There were also escort carriers to provide close air support for the assault forces, adding another 450 planes to the U.S. fleet. The warships, transports, landing ships, and auxiliaries for the Philippine operation would number more than a thousand. The Fast Carrier Force itself included six fast battleships, 14 cruisers and 58 destroyers; a force of older battleships, many veterans of the Pearl Harbor attack, would provide gunfire support for the landings.

The Japanese high command made preparations to counter the U.S. assault with what remained of the Imperial Japanese Navy. By October 1944 the Japanese had nine aircraft carriers in service (other than escort carriers). The pioneer *Hosho* was relegated to training duties. The other flattops were the veteran *Junyo* and *Zuikaku*; the new sister ships *Amagi* and *Unryu* (17,150 tons with space for some 65 aircraft); and the battle-tested light carriers *Chitose*, *Chiyoda*, *Ryuho*, and *Zuiho*. The eight carriers could embark almost 400 aircraft. In addition, the battleships *Hyuga* and *Ise* had been partially converted, with a flight deck installed aft so that each could carry and catapult 22 aircraft.

By October 1944, however, there were neither aircraft nor trained pilots available for these carriers. The Japanese aircraft industry was unable to produce sufficient planes to replace the losses in the Marianas and the thousand planes lost to the September carrier raids in the Philippines; the experienced pilots were mostly gone; and the severe shortage of fuel in the home islands prevented training new pilots. Further, the *Amagi*

TBM-1C torpedo-bombers of VT-19 returning to the *Lexington* after a strike on Formosa, October 12, 1944. A SB2C-3 dive-bomber of VB-19 stays in front of the forward anti-aircraft 5 in/38 twin mount Mk 32. (National Archives)

The *Zuikaku* launches her *Tenzan* Mk 12 carrier-based torpedo-bomber (B6N2, Jill) in the Inland Sea of Seto in early autumm of 1944. (Kinema Club/Toho Film)

Tenzan Mk 12s of the 653rd *Kokutai*, fitted with 800 kg (1,764 lb) aerial torpedoes, undergo attack training over the Inland Sea in September 1944. (Kinema Culb/Toho Film)

and *Unryu* were not yet fully ready for sea, while the planes assigned to the carriers *Junyo* and *Ryuho* had been sent to Formosa to help ward off U.S. carrier strikes. Thus, for the last carrier battle of the war only four carriers and the two converted battleships were available to the Japanese.

The U.S. fast carriers first struck Formosa and then swung around to support the Philippine landings. On October 17, U.S. Army Rangers began landing on small islands in the Leyte Gulf, the prelude to the main landings at Leyte. Offshore the fleets of transports and landing ships were assembling, with 18 escort carriers in three groups providing air patrols. Three of the larger CVEs each embarked 22 F6F Hellcats and 9 TBM Avengers; the others had 12 to 18 of the FM model of the Wildcat plus 9 TBF/TBM Avengers a total of some 450 aircraft.

In Tokyo the Japanese fleet commander gave the order to his forces to sortie to attack the U.S. forces off the Philippines. Three separate task forces would sail to engage the U.S. fleet. The First Diversion Attack Force (consisting of three groups as the First, the Second, and the Third Force) at Borneo had the largest concentration of battleships and cruisers yet assembled by any nation in the war: there were seven battleships, including the 64,000-ton behemoths *Yamato* and *Musashi*; 11 heavy and 2 light cruisers; and 19 destroyers. At the same time, the Second Diversion Attack Force sortied from Formosa with 2 heavy cruisers, 1 light cruiser, and 4 destroyers.

This mighty battle force was to pass through the Philippine islands, exit the San Bernardino Strait, and turn south to fall on the U.S. transports and landing ships. However, en route to the Philippines the First Diversion Attack Force would split off the Third Force with two battleships, a heavy cruiser, and four destroyers to take a southern channel through the islands; the Second Diversion Attack Force, with seven ships, would follow this route.

The so-called Main Body of Mobile Force, departing Japan's Inland Sea, had four carriers—the *Zuikaku*, *Chitose*, *Chiyoda*, and *Zuiho*, plus the two carrier-battleships and a screen of 3 light cruisers and 8 destroyers. They would steam south to launch air strikes and divert the U.S. carriers away from the beachhead so that the big-gun ships could attack the transports. On the decks of the four Japanese carriers were 116 aircraft: 52 Zero fighters, 28 Zero fighter-bombers, 7 Judy dive

bombers, and 25 Jill and 4 Kate torpedo planes. These aircraft—less than one-tenth the number in the U.S. fast carriers—were all that remained of the vaunted Japanese carrier fleet. While the battle forces approached the beachhead, the Main Body's four carriers would decoy the U.S. fast carriers away from the beachhead.

The battle again began with U.S. submarines drawing the first blood. The submarines sighted and tracked the First Diversion Attack Force, torpedoing and sinking two heavy cruisers and damaging a third. When the U.S. Fast Carrier Force was alerted one carrier task group was en route to Ulithi to replenish. The three remaining groups—with 12 carriers—were ordered to close with the Philippines and fly off searches. They did so at dawn of the October 24, and at 8:12 a plane from the *Intrepid* sighted 27 Japanese warships in the Sibuyan Sea steaming toward the San Bernardino Strait. A few minutes later a smaller group of seven Japanese ships was sighted steaming through the Philippines. The U.S. fleet commander, Admiral William F.(Bull) Halsey, ordered the carriers to attack.

Unknown to the Americans, during the night the Japanese had shifted several hundred aircraft from Formosa to the Philippines. On the morning of October 24 these planes began raids against the U.S. fast carriers operating offshore. Three waves, each of 50 to 60 aircraft, were the first to seek out the U.S. carriers. Most of the attackers were easily shot down by the F6F Hellcats before they could reach the U.S. ships; but at 9:38 a.m. a lone Judy dive bomber streaked out of the clouds and released two 250 kg (551 lb) bombs over the light carrier *Princeton*.

The bombs smashed through three decks of the unarmored ship before exploding. Three Avengers in the hangar, armed with torpedoes, were enveloped in flames and exploded. Men not fighting the flames were ordered off the ship. The fight to save the *Princeton* continued into the afternoon until, with the cruiser *Birmingham* alongside to help fight the fires, the carrier blew up at 3:23 p.m. The explosion and flying debris killed 229 men on the deck of the cruiser and injured another 420, some of whom would not survive. The *Birmingham*, her decks running with blood, pulled away.

Still, the *Princeton* remained afloat although her interior had been gutted. At 4 p.m. she was ordered abandoned.

U.S. ships fired several torpedoes into the light carrier to end her agony. The *Princeton* was the first U.S. fast carrier sunk since the *Hornet* (CV-8) had gone down two years before in the Solomons. Only 116 were killed in the *Princeton* of the 1,500-man crew. On board about to take command when she was hit was Captain John M. Hoskins; his right foot was mangled in the explosions and had to be amputated; he would survive and after the war go on to command a new carrier given the name *Princeton* (CV-37).

Even as the *Princeton* was in her agony, the 11 other carriers were attacking the Japanese surface forces coming through the Sibuyan Sea. A first strike of 259 fighters and bombers were sent off and found the Japanese group containing the *Yamato* and *Musashi*, three other battleships, nine cruisers, and 13 destroyers. The two super-dreadnoughts opened fire against the aircraft with the 18.1 in (46 cm) main batteries as well as their massive anti-aircraft batteries of more than 100 guns per ship. At 10:27 the *Musashi* was struck by a bomb and a torpedo, which inflicted little damage. A short while later she was hit again—by six more bombs and eight more torpedoes. The giant was slowed, in part by flooding (some intentional to balance flooding from torpedo damage), but she continued on with the other ships. U.S. air strikes continued throughout the day, and beginning about 3:30 the *Musashi* was hit by eleven more torpedoes and another ten bombs.

The flooding soon became uncontrollable and, after attempts to beach the *Musashi* failed, she was abandoned. Of 2,399 men on board, 1,023 were lost when the giant rolled over and sank at about 7:35 p.m. Several other ships were hit; the Japanese force reversed course, away from the San Bernardino Strait. It had taken 20 torpedo hits and 17 bombs to destroy the *Musashi*. On the U.S. side the attacks had cost the fast carriers only 18 planes in combat plus two operational losses. Including 10 planes lost in air patrols and searches, and 26 that went down with the *Princeton*, the total losses for the opening day of the fleet action were 56 U.S. carrier planes, and they would be quickly replaced by the shuttle of "jeep" carriers that brought out replacement planes and pilots. Even the loss of the *Princeton* would have virtually no affect on the U.S. carrier force.

Also on October 24, the Third Force with two battleships headed for Leyte Gulf through the Surigao Strait. U.S. search planes had found these ships on the afternoon of the 24th, and several bomb hits had been scored by the succeeding carrier strike. But this action was broken off to concentrate aircraft against the larger, *Yamato-Musashi* force in the Sibuyan Sea. Forewarned of the seven approaching Japanese warships, the commander of the U.S. assault force set a trap in the narrow Surigao Strait—hordes of U.S. torpedo boats, light cruisers, and then six older battleships were positioned for a night engagement. That night, in history's last battleship-versus-battleship combat, the two Japanese battleships and two destroyers were sunk; the heavy cruiser and destroyer were badly damaged, leaving only one destroyer intact. These ships were followed into the American trap by the Second Diversion Attack Force; this force,

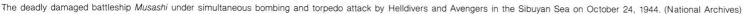

The deadly damaged battleship *Musashi* under simultaneous bombing and torpedo attack by Helldivers and Avengers in the Sibuyan Sea on October 24, 1944. (National Archives)

Grumman/General Motors (Eastern Division) TBM-1C Avenger flying over the Japanese battleship *Yamato* on October 24, 1944, during the Battle for Leyte Gulf.

1 Spinner
2 Propeller hub pitch change mechanism
3 Hamilton-Standard hydromatic constant-speed propeller (diameter: 13 ft/3.96 m)
4 Reduction gearbox
5 Carburetor air intake
6 Carburetor air trunking
7 Wright R-2600-8 14-cylinder two-row radial air-cooled engine (1,700 hp for take-off)
8 Cowl flaps
9 Cowl flap control lever
10 Exhaust pipe
11 Oil cooler
12 Oil cooler air exit flap
13 Mk 13-2 aerial torpedo
14 Bomb bay door
15 Twin carburetors

16 Engine control rods
17 Engine support struts
18 Oil tank (13 U.S. gal/49 ltr)
19 Oil filler cap
20 Firewall
21 AN-N6 gun camera
22 Ring & bead gunsight
23 Mk 8 gun/torpedo sight
24 Instrument panel shroud
25 Back of instrument panel
26 Rudder pedal
27 Throttle lever
28 Aileron tab control
29 Rudder tab control
30 Tail wheel caster lock
31 Armrest
32 Pilot's seat
33 Seat-back armor
34 Headrest
35 Main landing gear retraction jack

36 Wing fold locking cylinder
37 Mainwheel oleo leg
38 Machine gun blast tube
39 Torque links
40 Removable wheel disc cover
41 Tire
42 ASB-3 radar antennas
43 Fixed leading edge slots
44 Running light (red)
45 Pitot tube
46 Aileron trim tab
47 Trim tab control rod
48 Aileron control mechanism
49 Aileron structure
50 Ammunition magazine (280 rounds)
51 Flap control mechanism
52 Ammunition feed chute (40 rounds)
53 Main spar
54 0.50 in (12.7 mm)
   Browning M2 machine gun
55 Torpedo stabilizer

56 Left internal wing tank (90 U.S. gal/341 ltr)
57 Elevator servo motor
58 Aileron servo motor
59 Oxygen bottle
60 Flight indicator
61 Banking motor
62 Rudder servo motor
63 Accumulator
64 Hydraulic reservoir
65 ASB equipment
66 Crash bulkhead
67 Formation bombing
   visual salvo release signal
68 Recognition light
69 Antenna mast
70 Antenna
71 Turret enclosure
72 Gunner's armored seat
73 0.50 in (12.7 mm) Browning M2
   machine gun (400 rounds)
74 Main control unit
75 Firing grip

76 ASB aiming controller
77 Transmitter
78 Bomber's seat
79 Antenna reel
80 Antenna fairlead
81 Bomber's window
82 0.30 in (7.62 mm) Browning M2 (M1919A2)
   machine gun (500 rounds)
83 Spare coil containers
84 Parachute flare containers
85 Armor plate supports
86 Section light (blue)
87 Float lights rack
88 Tailwheel retracting mechanism
89 Hydraulic actuating strut
90 Lifting tube
91 Oleo strut
92 Tailwheel
93 Arresting hook retraction drive motor
94 Elevator/Rudder control cables
95 Arresting hook guide rails
96 Arresting hook
97 Aileron structure
98 Elevator trim tab
99 Trim tab control rod
100 Rudder trim tab
101 Rudder structure
102 Tail ranning light (white)
103 Antenna rear mounting

Torpedo-armed *Tenzan* Mk 12 (Jill) takes off from the carrier *Zuikaku* in early autumn of 1944. (Kinema Club/Toho Film)

TBM-1C of the *San Jacinto*'s VT-51 is armed with a Mk 13 torpedo in preparation for a strike on Japanese carriers, October 25, 1944. (National Archives)

more astutely handled, suffered minor damage (one ship in a collision with the already damaged cruiser) and fled in retreat. The only American losses in this phase of the battle was a destroyer shot up (by friendly forces) and several torpedo boats damaged. The next morning aircraft from the U.S. escort carriers in Leyte Gulf sufficiently damaged a heavy cruiser so that she had to be scuttled.

Thus, from the U.S. perspective, both Japanese attempts to penetrate to Leyte Gulf with surface forces had been turned back. The presence of the Main Body with four carriers was still unknown to the Americans. On the morning of the 24th the Japanese ships launched a small air strike against the U.S. carriers that was easily beaten off; the survivors flew into airfields on Leyte. Although the approach of the Japanese planes had revealed the threat from the northwest, the U.S. carrier force was too busy attacking the *Yamato-Musashi* force, and not until 4:40 p.m. were the Japanese carriers sighted, only

190 miles (350 km) from the northernmost U.S. carrier group. Admiral Halsey, who had rejoined the Fast Carrier Force, turned three carrier groups northward for a dawn attack against the Japanese carriers. At the same time, Halsey withdrew his six fast battleships (including his own flagship *New Jersey*) from the carrier group and formed them in a battle group ahead of the U.S. carriers as the force steamed toward the Japanese carriers.

At first light on the 25th, U.S. ships flew off search planes followed by a strike of 180 aircraft. At 7:35 a.m. the Japanese carriers were sighted, and the last carrier-versus-carrier battle of the war began. The defending Zeros were brushed aside, and despite heavy anti-aircraft fire from the 17 Japanese ships, the bomb-armed Helldivers and Avenger torpedo planes bore into their targets. The first carrier to go under was the *Chitose* which took several bomb hits in the first strike; she sunk at 9:37 a.m. The large *Zuikaku*—the last survivor of

The end of the veteran *Zuikaku*. Crew members give three cheers on the heavily listing deck on October 25, 1944. (Yoji Watanabe)

The burning light carrier *Zuiho* maneuvers to escape further blows. The photograph was taken by an Avenger torpedo plane on October 25. (National Archives)

the six carriers at Pearl Harbor—suffered a torpedo hit, and a single bomb from this strike hit the *Zuiho*. A destroyer was also sunk.

A short time later a small strike of only 36 U.S. carrier planes reached the scene. These planes inflicted severe damage on the *Chiyoda* and she was taken in tow.

The third strike, with more than 200 planes, sent seven torpedoes and four bombs into the *Zuikaku*, and she began to sink, going under at 2:14 p.m. The smaller *Zuiho* was also hit and set on fire, but she was able to survive this strike.

A fourth strike of 35 carrier aircraft concentrated on the damaged *Zuiho*, and she sank at 3:26 p.m. A fifth strike of 96 planes reached the surviving Japanese ships at 5 p.m. but inflicted no significant damage. The sixth (and final) strike of 36 planes also caused little damage. Some of the U.S. carrier pilots has flown three missions during the day to sink three carriers and damage a fourth.

The light carrier *Chiyoda* remained afloat, dead in the water. Also surviving were the two flight-deck battleships and nine smaller warships. These ships were spread out over the area. Racing ahead of the U.S. carriers, a cruiser-destroyer group reached the crippled *Chiyoda*. At 4:25 p.m. the ships opened fire and 30 minutes later she too went down, the fourth Japanese carrier to die in the battle. After dark, guided by carrier planes, these ships also sank a destroyer.

Meanwhile, a near-disaster was befalling the U.S. amphibious force off Leyte Gulf. Late on October 24, after losing the *Musashi* to U.S. carrier attacks and reversing course, the Japanese force again changed course—toward San Bernardino Strait. There were still the *Yamato* and three other battleships, eight cruisers, and 13 destroyers in the force. At 6:45 a.m. the northernmost of the U.S. escort carriers off Leyte Gulf sighted anti-aircraft shell bursts to the north. A short time later the pagoda masts of Japanese ships were visible. The Japanese battle force broke through San Bernardino and found the three U.S. carrier groups—18 thin-skin escort carriers, 9 destroyers, and 14 destroyer escorts. The CVEs, intended to provide close air support to troops ashore, had no armor-piercing bombs or torpedoes in their magazines.

The Japanese ships began firing at 6:48 a.m. The destroyers and escorts laid smoke and then attacked the Japanese ships. But they were undergunned, and two destroyers and an escort were sunk and others were hit without inflicting damage on the Japanese ships. Meanwhile, the battleship and cruiser guns

scored hit after hit on the escort carriers. The *Gambier Bay* (CVE-73) went down with about 100 of her 850-man crew. Remarkably, the four other CVEs hit by battleship and cruiser fire survived, although heavily damaged.

The Japanese force was also taken by surprise in the encounter. The ferocity of the attacks by the escort carriers' planes—with machine guns, rockets, and depth charges—and damage to three of his cruisers by the U.S. ships convinced the Japanese commander to break off the engagement. He withdrew his ships, after scuttling the three damaged cruisers.

The ordeal of the escort carriers was not yet over. On that day—October 25, 1944—the Japanese aircraft flying from the Philippines initiated the *kamikaze* suicide attacks. The suiciders struck several of the escort carriers, one of which was almost simultaneously hit by a torpedo fired by a Japanese submarine; that ship survived. Only one CVE was sunk by the *kamikaze* attackers and several more damaged.

Meanwhile, the battleship attacks had forced Admiral Halsey to turn most of his carriers and his fast battleships south. Instead of finishing off the *Ise* and *Hyuga*, his ships steamed toward the escort carriers. They arrived too late to attack the fleeing ships, and the Battles of Leyte Gulf were at an end, as was the Japanese carrier force. In the series of engagements the Japanese had lost four carriers, three battleships, and 17 other warships; the battles cost the U.S. Navy only one light carrier, two CVEs, and a few lesser ships sunk.

The Japanese fleet had in reality ceased to exist. There were many large warships and several carriers still flying the ensign of the Rising Sun. Most were anchored in Japanese home waters, their fuel bunkers empty because of the interdiction of tanker routes by U.S. submarines. Among the carriers in home waters was the 62,000-ton *Shinano*, the largest carrier yet constructed by any nation. She was launched on November 11, 1944. Early on the morning of the 30th of that month she was steaming on her maiden voyage off Tokyo Bay when the U.S. submarine *Archerfish* sighted her. Firing a spread of six torpedoes, the submarine hit her with four, and later that morning, without ever having flown aircraft, the giant carrier sank beneath the sea. In December 1944 two U.S. submarines severely damaged the *Junyo*; she limped into port and never returned to sea. Later in the month one of those submarines torpedoed and sank the *Unryu*.

There would be no more carrier battles for the U.S. Fast Carrier Force. The fast carriers—reinforced from March

The last fight of the mightiest Japanese battleship *Yamato* against U.S. carrier air power on April 7, 1945. Two of eight escort destroyers, the *Fuyuzuki* (left) and *Hatsushimo* (right) are seen around the *Yamato*. (National Archives)

1945 by four British armored-deck carriers—struck targets ashore. After the Philippines campaign, the Americans assaulted Okinawa and then Iwo Jima. The fast carriers provided direct support of these landings, diversionary raids throughout the remainder of the Japanese Empire, and beginning on February 16, 1945, attacked the Japanese home islands. The carrier force that came to Japan numbered 116 warships, including 11 large and 5 light carriers as well as 8 fast battleships. Of the flattops, only the *Enterprise* and *Saratoga* had been in commission when the war began.

The only significant opposition to this armada was the aerial *kamikaze* attacks. Admiral Halsey called the suiciders the only thing that frightened him during the war. Even they, however, could not stop the fast carriers. Several carriers were heavily damaged by suiciders as well as conventional bombing attacks, but none was sunk. All were repaired, although two, the *Bunker hill* and *Franklin* did not return to service.

The carriers struck Japanese airfields and troop concentrations, factories and storage depots, and warships at anchor in bays and coves of the Inland Sea. There was but one major Japanese ship attacked at sea—the super-battleship *Yamato*. On April 1, 1944, U.S. troops landed on Okinawa; on April 6 the *Yamato* sailed from Mitajiri for Okinawa. She carried enough fuel for a one-way trip. The ship was to reach the beachhead and destroy American transports. With 2,774 men on board, she was the largest *kamikaze* of all. A light cruiser and eight destroyers sailed with her.

U.S. submarines trailed the Japanese ships and alerted the U.S. commanders. At 8:27 a.m. on April 7 a search plane from the carrier *Essex* found the *Yamato* and an hour later the fast carriers began launching a 280-plane strike. Of the planes, however, 53 planes from the *Hancock* were late taking off and never found their target. A second strike with 106 planes was flown off a short time later.

At 12:32 the *Yamato* began firing at the approaching planes with her 18.1 in (46 cm) guns. Moments later all guns of the force commenced firing. The battleship alone had 24 5 in (12.7 cm) guns and some 150 25 mm guns. The carrier planes

were not deterred. The battleship survived less than two hours; struck by only five bombs and ten torpedoes; at 2:23 the ship sank, with her magazines exploding after she had gone under. The carrier planes easily sank the light cruiser as well as four of the destroyers.

The war in the Pacific continued for four more months. Japan capitulated in mid-August and U.S. warships entered Japanese home waters. Much of the American armada was anchored in Tokyo Bay on September 2, 1945, when, on the deck of the battleship *Missouri*, the surrender documents were signed. The U.S. fast carriers remained at sea. Admiral Halsey believed in "playing it safe," just in case the surrender was some sort of ghastly trick. At the moment the ceremonies were ended, all present looked skyward as wave after wave of carrier planes—one thousand aircraft— flew overhead.

It was a fitting conclusion to the ceremonies. The war in the Atlantic, the Mediterranean, on the Murmansk run, and across the broad Pacific had, in large part, been a carrier war.

The remains of the Japanese carrier force. The wrecked new carrier *Amagi* rests on the bottom near Kure Naval Base on October 8, 1945. (National Archives)